PRAISE FOR
HOPE AT WORK
(IN ALPHABETICAL ORDER)

"I do not use the word hope on a regular basis, but I practiced it every day as a leader and CEO. Where hope is concerned, it is **what you do** that matters, not what you say or think you are doing. *Hope at Work* works for me."

ARON AIN, Former CEO and Chairman, UKG

"If you act, it means you have hope. In a world where my generation, and likely the next, will face deep uncertainty, that reminder matters. Harry and Barbara revisit the idea of hope with fresh clarity, offering insights and more importantly, sharing stories that show why hope remains the force that enables us to build a better world."

BERAT EFE ALKAN, Entrepreneur, Istanbul
(INSEAD MBA '27J)

"Haiti has changed me. Haitians have shown me that even in hardship, there is always hope. This book tells my story."

MICHAEL ANELLO, Executive Director, Haiti Reforestation Partnership

"Perry and Hutson deliver twenty years of proof that hope isn't soft; it's structural. *Hope at Work* shows how organizations that choose hope don›t just adapt, they outperform. If you believe the next decade demands more than efficiency, start here."

DOUGLAS ANWEILER, Chief Strategist, Bellwoods Strategy, Toronto

"In my work on the Hope Gap, I've learned that hope isn't naïve—it's a strategic force that moves people from despair to possibility. *Hope at Work* gives leaders the tools to activate that shift. It turns hope into a practical framework for culture, connection, and meaningful, measurable change."

AFDHEL AZIZ, Chief Purpose Officer,
Good Is the New Cool + Conspiracy of Love

"This is an extraordinary book about a topic we all need to be talking about: the power of hope in the workplace. Every chapter is packed with illuminating (and practical) examples of how leaders and communities are using evidence-based tools to actively choose hope and, as a result, drive real transformation. Before I opened the book, I hadn't thought about how hope could be harnessed, in a systematic way, for positive change throughout an organization. Now it's <u>all</u> I can think about."

SCOTT CAMERON, Executive Producer,
International Sesame Street

"This book lights the way toward hope with actionable strategies and vivid, real-world examples, offering inspiration and practical guidance for anyone seeking a brighter path forward. Its message is uplifting, and its real-world examples are both aspirational and achievable. Discover how five principles of hope can transform uncertainty into possibility and create a future worth believing in."

GAIL VANCE CIVILLE, Founder and CEO,
Sensory Spectrum

"In *Hope at Work*, Barbara Perry and Harry Hutson offer organizations a gift we urgently need: a framework for turning hope from sentiment into a shared capability—a disciplined, collective practice that fuels belonging, resilience, and meaningful progress. Their five principles remind us that hope isn't naïveté or avoidance, but a courageous engagement with what is and what could be, enacted through agency, connection, and a deep sense of worth. As I've learned in my own work, hope is the quiet engine of redemption—the refusal to let despair have the last word. This book shows leaders how to nurture that engine in themselves and in their teams, making a better future possible and reminding us that, yes, hope is the most important decision we can make."

JERRY COLONNA, CEO of Reboot.io;
Author of *Reboot* and *Reunion*

"Barbara and Harry have given us a gift that is inspiring and indispensable as we work to help ourselves and others "activate agency" and cultivate possibility. *Hope at Work* is rich in insight and alive with tangible life lessons."

DAVID DODSON, Philanthropist and Nonprofit Trustee

"When American society has thrived—the Revolutionary period, the Progressive Era, the Civil Rights Era—the force of hope has won against armies of despair, cynicism, and impotence. We have entered a downward spiral in our current society, and the Perry-Hutson book offers us a very practical, believable way to escape, to resume our positive journey. The application of their methods in small and large ways opens the way."

BARRY DYM, Psychotherapist, Organizational
Consultant and Social Activist

"Rarely does a book so elegantly balance human-centered values with strategic rigor. The 5 Principles offer a clear path to transform uncertainty into possibility. From their depth of experience, Perry and Hutson provide essential insight for every new age leader and consultant."

NIKITA (YOGI) GANATRA, Organization Development Consultant and Coach; Research Scholar at Manipal University, Jaipur

"This book is exactly what the world, and today's organizations need more of. Hope is the soul of successful teams, enduring strategies, and a leader's lasting legacy. This is a remarkable testament to how hope unlocks human and organizational potential."

SHANNON GARCIA, Global Company President

"Dynamic 'hopester' duo, Barbara and Harry, have done it again. I was hooked in just the first few pages of the Introduction. This collection and advocacy of compelling evidence firmly plants Hope as necessary pillar and virtue for any leader in every organization. The wisdom, guidance, and encouragement from this book are a gift to leaders everywhere. Filled with impactful stories, transparent anecdotes, memorable quotes and practical applications, this book will become an active, inspiring resource in my daily life, rather than a nice once-and-done read. I'd love to see this book in the hands of every leader in my life—past, present and future."

TROY GEESAMAN, SVP at Seed Strategy; Instructor. Cox School of Business, Southern Methodist University

"More than a business consulting book, Barbara Perry and Harry Hutson bring us a richly informed treatise on a key driver of individual and organizational health and flourishing in contexts from surgical suites or concert halls to boardrooms. Drawing upon their own diverse and extensive experience in consulting, the lessons of the social science disciplines, the wisdom of the ancients, spiritual teachers, philosophers, and difference-makers throughout history, they lead us to a deeper understanding and appreciation of hope. They teach us what hope is, and what it is not, and structure their treatise around its essential principles. In a work that engagingly balances scholarship with story they show us that hope is an essential human ingredient at the core of our lives and how, when embraced, it can bind groups in concrete action to realize a better future."

MARK GIBSON, MD, Physician and Medical Educator

"*Hope at Work* turns hope into the leadership practice that we all need in 2026. This book makes the most practical and timely case for hope I've seen in years. It treats hope not as a mood, but as an operational capability that leaders can build, measure, and scale. The principles offer a clear architecture for cultures that perform under pressure without losing their humanity. What I appreciate most is the insistence on grounded hope: truth-telling, shared context, and the daily choices that turn uncertainty into forward motion. If you lead a team, a classroom, a clinic, or a community, you'll find a playbook that strengthens outcomes and restores meaning. I am gifting this book to our whole team!"

DANA GRIFFIN, Co-Founder and CEO, Eldera.ai

"When Barbara and Harry first reached out with their book idea, I was a bit unsure how I could lend any valuable perspective to the concept of hope (I really hadn't thought much about it); but their curiosity and dedication drew me in. What they've produced is a brilliant guide that takes hope from a passive feeling into a collective force for systemic change. Their framework of the Five Principles—how we Explore Possibility, Activate Agency, Uphold Worth, Embrace Openness, and Establish Connection—offers a practical roadmap for cultivating resilience and high performance. Their work is a profound statement that, even in turbulent times, choosing hope is the most strategic business decision an organization can make."

JAY HASBROUCK, Applied Anthropologist and Author

"As a Regional Vice President responsible for 800 stores and 18,000 partners, I saw firsthand that hope is not delivered through strategy it is created through presence. Post-Covid, I was asked by Howard Schultz to travel the country with other leaders to listen deeply to partners' lived experiences. What we heard was not a demand for certainty, but a longing to be acknowledged, understood, and believed in. When partners felt truly heard, something shifted. Hope surfaced, not as optimism, but as possibility. Through honest, hope-filled dialogue, partners opened themselves to what could be rebuilt together. In those moments, listening became an act of leadership, and hope became a shared discipline rather than a message from above. Hope was not something we gave our partners. It was something we uncovered with them, one conversation at a time."

CAMILLE HYMES, Former Starbucks Executive; COO, Smoothie King

"Today's workplace can feel relentlessly chaotic—shaped by COVID and return-to-office transitions, layoffs, hard conversations about compensation and promotion, fewer resources but higher demands, and now the rise of AI. *Hope at Work* has been my anchor in those moments. It offers a blueprint for leading with empathy and clarity, without compromising excellence. Hope steadies us. It grounds the work. It reminds us what we're here to do—and who we're doing it for."
 NICHOLAS INCORVAIA, Creative Marketing Leader, Amazon

"*Hope at Work* shows that when people feel valued, connected, and capable of shaping what comes next, the unimaginable happens. Hope fuels resilience, restores energy, and turns everyday work into something that touches the soul."
 DeSHONNE JACKSON, VP, Stores and Services North America, Nike

"At a time when the 'hope gap' seems to widen daily in our work and in our lives, Barbara and Harry provide a grounded and thoughtful meditation on why it is important to inspire and sustain hope. Their analysis delineates the need for and power of organizations and communities that inspire possibility, fuel our sense of agency, honor our worth, create space for openness and foster deeper, more meaningful connections."
 KEVIN JORDAN, Career Architect, Leadership Catalyst and Principal, Kevin Jordan Coach

"Today, we need hope more than ever in our homes, communities and workplaces. In *Hope at Work*, authors Barbara Perry and Harry Hutson go beyond advocacy to create a model for instilling hope in the workplace. Through research and case studies, they show how leaders can embed hope into culture, decision-making, and relationships. Ultimately, the book provides a much-needed framework for leaders to intentionally cultivate hope to make a better future possible."

CURTIS KOPF, Digital and Customer Experience Leader; Author, *In Pursuit of the Customer*

"In my work listening to and researching younger generations, I see a quiet tension: many feel stuck, yet deeply long for a life that feels alive and meaningful. This book is a gentle yet firm reminder: hope is the kind of magic that turns a caterpillar into a butterfly. Through powerful, true stories across different organizations and contexts, it shows that hope is much like breathing—often invisible, yet profoundly present. A living, regenerative force that creates possibility, invites action, and opens space for new potential to emerge. How wonderful it is to keep hope alive."

LYNN LIN, Co-founder of FuturistCircle, Shanghai

"Twenty years on from *Putting Hope to Work*, the concepts and principles are more relevant than ever. At Touch, we exist to remind business of its core: people. Without them, nothing else matters. That's why we balance empathy, awareness, understanding—and hope—as active strategies alongside the practical realities of budgets, hiring, growth and sales. Hope unlocks innovation, fuels connection, and drives the actions that create real change in the world."

BRAD MACE, Principal, TouchWorldwide

"People do their best work and organizations thrive when leaders show they care. Employees are energized by a world of possibilities, the chance to contribute and make a meaningful difference. And having, feeling and seeing hope at work is the foundation."

CHRISTINE McHUGH, Christine McHugh Consulting

"I love this book. It is beautiful and written in a way that translates years of observation, research and stories about hope in the workplace into something interesting, provocative, usable, and potentially powerful. Barbara Perry and Harry Hutson know hope, defining what it is and why it matters. What sets their book apart is the *how*: practices, discipline and action to enable you to lead with hope. What if the organization you lead was known as a hopeful place, where hope is a way of being, where hope means being seen and heard, where folks are engaged in intentionally and intensely exploring "Why not?" "What's next?" "What if?" Where hope means transparency, listening with care, curiosity, and commitment. Where hope means excellence in results and in who we are as human beings. What if we can we truly change things? The wisdom and practicality in this book can change the way we live our lives, lead our organizations and light our world."

EDNA MORRIS, Investor, Leader, Advisor; Board Chair, Tractor Supply Company

"I've lived this work. I've seen what happens when people begin to believe in a better future and feel equipped to shape it. *Hope at Work* shows leaders how to create those conditions—consistently, courageously, and at every level of an organization. In a world defined by complexity and almost constant change, this is the kind of leadership we need now more than ever."

DENISE NELSEN, Co-Architect and Board Member, SGNL Advisory

"*Hope at Work* is an important reminder that organizations don't succeed on strategy and finance alone. They succeed when people believe their work matters, when they feel agency rather than fear, and when leaders take responsibility for creating *meaning*, not just managing outcomes. This is a serious and timely book about the moral work of leadership."

      MARK D. NEVINS, President, Nevins Consulting

"Where does hope come from? When hope is gone, where does it go and how do we bring it back?... *Hope at Work: 5 Principles to Breathe Life into Your Organization* is uplifting by helping the reader understand how to encourage leaders to choose hope and overcome challenges through storytelling, intense listening, relationship building and drawing on the legacies of our ancestors. The authors' personal and sometimes vulnerable approach makes clear there is no hope without conflict and more importantly the willingness to work through it. They highlight hope's role during uncertain times by offering tools anyone at all levels can use to nurture and invite hope's presence without requiring special programs. Hope isn't just a feel-good thing; it's an essential ingredient for any successful organization."

      RICHARD L. O'BRYANT, Chief Belonging Officer
and Director, the John D. O'Bryant African American Institute,
             Northeastern University

"In my experience, business books offer practical advice or inspiration but rarely both. *Hope at Work* delivers motivation coupled with the key elements you need to foster a culture of hope, the kind of culture that creates team engagement and tremendous outcomes. Barb and Harry are an equally rare combination of talents and their experience in working with some of the most innovative organizations shines through. Hope IS the essential underpinning of resilient cultures. *Hope at Work* will inspire and equip you to lead with possibility and confidence."

DENNY POST, Director, *Travel + Leisure* and Vital Farms

"What an unexpected, thoughtful, and provocative book! Grounded in research, experience, and real-life examples, Perry and Hutson connect concepts to business realities, tangible outcomes, and people. They successfully make the business case for hope-filled leadership—a 'way to name what really matters, rally others… and sustain shared momentum' to define the future and achieve your business vision. Importantly, the authors provide leaders in every organization a simple, clear, roadmap to build cultures where people not only believe in the future but also take specific steps to make it real."

TARA RETHORE, Global Executive Coach and CEO, Strategy For Real™

"*Hope at Work* isn't a book about pep talks or positive thinking. It's a book about the deeper human architecture inside every leader. It reminds us that hope isn't a mood—it's a discipline of clarity, courage, and connection. When leaders do the inner work of knowing themselves, they awaken the same truth in others. That's the real work of leadership today, and this book sits at the center of that conversation."

MIKE RITZ, Cross-Sector Leadership Strategist

"In *Hope at Work*, Barbara Perry and Harry Hutson have issued a clarion call to leaders to create organizational cultures of hope which inspire individuals and institutions to seize the moment to shape a more positive future. *Hope at Work* is not only compelling in content but is well researched and presented in an easily readable style, celebrating the importance of storytelling."

BOB ROSS, former CEO, St. Joseph's
Addiction Treatment and Recovery Centers

"*Hope at Work* is essential reading for anyone committed to culture, leadership, and lasting performance. In a world defined by uncertainty, it offers clarity, courage, and a practical roadmap for creating workplaces where people genuinely thrive."

NAVEEN SANDERS, Global CXO and
"A Champion of Hope"

"On my leadership journey, I've had the privilege of learning about *Hope at Work*, and the impact on my thinking was immediate and profound. I had always viewed hope as a feeling—something you simply carried. What this book reveals, with clarity and compassion, is that hope is a practiced discipline built on principles that can be taught, tested, and lived. The framework of possibility, agency, worth, openness, and connection reshaped how I lead and how I help others find their footing in complex times. This is a powerful, practical guide for anyone committed to creating a workplace where people can move forward with purpose and resilience."

DEBBIE STROUD, President & CEO, Whataburger

"For anyone skeptical of hope, look no further. *Hope at Work* shows that hope is not wishful thinking but a proven, rigorous, and actionable leadership practice. In a world changing at extraordinary speed—when humanity matters more than ever—this book empowers people in their own lives and shows how hope, once activated, creates ripple effects that strengthen families, teams and organizations."

VIRGINIA TENPENNY, VP Community Impact, HCA Healthcare

"*Hope at Work* captures the leadership I believe in, not certainty, but possibility—inviting people into a future they can actually reach. Barbara Perry and Harry Hutson turn hope from a poster word into practical, everyday work—powered by curiosity, agency, and connection. It's the kind of book that builds cultures that are worth belonging, to and results that are worth trusting."

MICHELLE WICKHAM, VP National Operations, Scooter's Coffee

"Hope as a practice builds a culture where belief systems produce outcomes only achieved through the collective engagement of people, teams and leaders. As we started on our journey of putting hope to work, we realized our conventional thinking of success was insufficient to measure the possibilities we uncovered. The absolute best part of our odyssey was witnessing the unlocking of human potential which changed all of our lives forever!"

ROSSANN WILLIAMS, Former EVP and President, Starbucks North American Retail

"I've been inspired by Barbara's work for more than three decades, and this book, with Harry, might be her most essential contribution yet. In a world being rapidly reshaped by AI and uncertainty, *Hope at Work* offers the human grounding leaders desperately need to build organizations where people can still see—and shape—a better future."

JOHN WINSOR, Founder and Chairman, Open Assembly; Executive Fellow Harvard Business School

HOPE AT WORK

Hope at Work
Copyright © 2026 by Barbara Perry and Harry Hutson

All rights reserved under the Pan-American and International Copyright Conventions. This book may not be reproduced in whole or in part, except for brief quotations embodied in critical articles or reviews, in any form or by any means, electronic or mechanical, including photocopying, recording, or by any information storage and retrieval system now known or hereinafter invented, without written permission of the publisher.

Information supplemental to the book's continents can be found here:

ISBN (paperback): 978-1-963271-68-3
ISBN (ebook): 978-1-963271-69-0

Armin Lear Press, Inc.
215 W Riverside Drive, #4362
Estes Park, CO 80517

HOPE AT WORK

5 Principles to Breathe Life into Your Organization

Barbara Perry & Harry Hutson

Barbara's Dedication:
To all of you on the front lines of hope. Thank you.

Harry's Dedication:
To Robert H. Schaffer, thought leader, mentor and friend whose ideas on rapid results, demand making and accountability for performance have shaped our field.

CONTENTS

Foreword		i
Introduction		1
1	Choosing Hope	9
2	Hope's Rewards	31
3	Create Possibility	43
4	Activate Agency	63
5	Uphold Worth	79
6	Embrace Openness	101
7	Establish Connection	123
8	Who Hopeful Leaders Are	139
9	What Hopeful Leaders Do	145
10	How Leaders Keep Their Hope Alive	157
11	Tracking Signs of Hope at Work	163
12	Putting Hope to Work—Again	171
With Gratitude		175
About the Authors		177

FOREWORD

Barbara and Harry's book, *Hope at Work: 5 Principles to Breathe Life into Your Organization*, and their five actionable principles for improving leadership effectiveness, is a resource I wish had been available…

- In 1983, when I was asked to lead Procter and Gamble's struggling Tide brand, which was at its lowest point since its launch in 1946,

- In 1993, when I was asked to get the Asia Pacific and Japan businesses growing. At the time, P&G's only truly profitable business in Japan was barely breaking even, and P&G's China business was not getting off the ground and was hemorrhaging losses,

- In 2000, when I was elected P&G's "accidental CEO" after the company's stock price and market capitalization had fallen by more than half,

- In 2013, when I was called back to P&G to help the team lead another turnaround, and,

- Many times, over the last ten years after retiring from P&G, when I was helping to start a new company, fix a troubled one or get an underperforming nonprofit back on track.

I have authored and coauthored books—on innovation: *Game-Changer: How You Can Revenue Growth and Profit with Innovation,* with Ram Charan; and on strategy: *Playing to Win: How Strategy Really Works,* with Roger Martin. I have written *Harvard Business Review* articles on executive leadership, including "What Only the CEO Can Do," "Leaders Shouldn't Try to Do It All," and "I Think of My Failures as a Gift." I have shared five decades of leadership learning through Medium, podcasts, and a wide range of local, national and international media outlets.

My work has focused on what leaders *do* to improve effectiveness. The right things they do to accomplish the mission, deliver results, and win. It reflects what my mentor, Peter Drucker, called the "effective practice of management."

That is what I value about *Hope at Work.*

The concepts are clear. The principles are proven. The real-world examples are easy to understand. Barbara and Harry have put together an approach and an action plan that can be put into practice. Their learnings are captured in stories that invite readers to apply the principles in their leadership circumstances.

They encourage leaders to search for opportunities to envision possibilities when problems seem overwhelming. To encourage individuals and teams to act and try different ways to deliver better outcomes. To reaffirm that the work being accomplished together is worth doing.

Barbara and Harry emphasize openness to change, to difference, and to learning from others inside and outside the organization: Teammates across businesses and functions. External partners who can influence results. Customers and suppliers, partners and investors, governments and regulators, and yes, even competitors and critics.

They also emphasize connection: grounding relationships in shared hope and mutual trust and combining complementary capabilities to improve collective performance.

To be clear, hope may or may not be a *strategy*.

Strategy is a coordinated and integrated set of choices that position a company to deliver better value for customers and greater value for employees and owners. Strategic choices about where to play and how to win must be supported by capabilities, resources and management systems that translate into actionable plans—and improve the odds of success.

But hope *is* a catalyst, a culture-builder, an enabler and an engine of higher individual, team and organizational performance. When cultivated and unleashed, hope becomes the force that empowers commitment and sustained performance.

It is remarkable what people can accomplish when they desire a certain outcome and share a belief that it can happen. It is equally remarkable what people accomplish when no one cares who gets the credit and then, once the goal is achieved, they say, "We did it! Together!"

As Barbara and Harry write, hope at work is a shared capacity to imagine and work toward a better future together. Companies and leaders who inspire hope have a better chance of unleashing the full potential of their teams and their total workforce.

I was not surprised by the 2025 Gallup poll results. When people were asked what they need most from their leaders, the answer was hope, followed by trust. Hope and trust are two sides of the same engaging, enabling, and empowering coin. Both are essential. And as trust in institutions and shared values declines, hope is one of the most powerful engagement levers leaders have today.

At P&G, integrity and trust, ownership and personal leadership—and winning with those who matter most—were core values. We believed the consumer is boss and employees are the company's most valuable resource.

In my judgment, the most effective leadership approach is to trust yourself, trust the team, and trust the organization. Remember this: You and they have been in more difficult situations than the one you are currently facing, and you succeeded.

P&G often performed best during crises. We were at greater risk of complacency when conditions were favorable. With hindsight, crises were opportunities to gain advantage and win bigger.

Outside P&G, I appeal to leaders to trust their values and principles, their capabilities and experience, their strategy and plans, and their proven ability to execute. I work to build confidence and courage of conviction based on evidence and prior success.

With hindsight, inspiring hope and trust in leaders, leadership teams and organizations offers the best chance of success. That is all a leader can do: Improve the odds. Nothing is guaranteed. Business and life are uncertain and risky.

Hope and trust make progress possible. Foster hope. Build trust. That may be the most effective one-two punch for leaders in 2026.

A.G. Lafley
January 2, 2026

INTRODUCTION

> "Grit depends on a different kind of hope. It rests on the expectation that our own efforts can improve our future."
>
> Angela Duckworth, author of *Grit: The Power of Passion and Perseverance*

Hope demands our attention. *Hope at Work* is our answer. This book distills and deepens *Putting Hope to Work: Five Principles to Activate Your Organization's Most Powerful Resource*, from 2006, with new evidence, more stories, and greater urgency.

The workplace is a crucible where the future is forged.

In a flourishing workplace, hope is a tool and a treasure.

Hope is essential. Especially now.

Fostering hope is recognized in organizational science as a strategic and evidence-based approach to enhancing both individual achievement and tangible outcomes. Leaders who intentionally cultivate hope create more positive work cultures and measurable improvements in outcomes that matter most. These are our headlines:

1. Hope Drives Performance: Hope is a key psychological resource that predicts higher engagement, resilience, goal orientation, productivity, and retention.

2. Hope Is a Buffer Against Stress and Burnout: Hopeful employees are less likely to experience burnout, even under pressure, because they believe in a better future and their ability to shape it.

3. Hope Signals Trust in Leadership and the Future: When employees feel hopeful, they tend to have stronger trust in leadership, a sense of progress, and emotional attachment to the organization.

4. Managers Are the Primary Carriers of Hope: Managers account for most of the variance in team engagement and are the key transmitters of hope through clarity, communication, empathy, and linking work to purpose.

5. Hope is Learnable, Actionable, and Measurable: Hope is not a vague feeling but a capability that can be measured, tracked, and linked to organizational outcomes.

In organizations around the world, we see a repeating pattern. When people lose hope, they withdraw, disconnect, or go through the motions. When hope is present, people engage. They experiment, invest, collaborate, and act.

Defining Hope

For decades, we have been observing hope at work. When we hear people talking about hope, we see how their words reach beyond themselves as solitary individuals. They point toward a stronger community, a safer workplace, a child's well-being, a team's breakthrough, a successful enterprise, a nation's healing. Hope is how we join one another in envisioning the possible and how we commit to making it happen. It lives in networks, partnerships, and teams. And when it begins in solitude, hope grows stronger when voiced and acted upon with others.

Our original definition of hope is still alive: At work, hope is the shared capacity of imagining and working toward a desirable future. As research on the efficacy of hope in organizations has continued to accumulate, we now define hope unreservedly:

Hope at Work Makes a Better Future Possible.

We hold that hope is causative and instrumental to progress. Hope belongs at work and is therefore a collective force. Hope is oriented toward reality, which we define as both what is and what can be. Organizational meaning is determined in interactions, and forward movement, especially in complex systems, requires collaboration and moral imagination.

We also assert that hope is not just a good feeling, a formula for success, or an antidote for hard times. Nor is hope a tactic in a playbook. Hope is a deep and universal need that is core to being human. It is a positive force in a weary world. When we talk about hope, we mean the kind that invites others in and thrives on what is shared.

The Five Principles of Hope

We became curious about hope in the early 1990's. Living in Boston, we began our search the old-fashioned way, in libraries. When we asked a librarian in the Widener Library at Harvard to do an interdisciplinary search on the topic of hope, she found little pertaining to hope in organizations. But she identified a trove of materials from collections of individual psychology, philosophy, theology, anthropology, poetry, and history—and of course mythology. Remember Pandora!

A literature search established our baseline as we began 30 years of field-based research. We worked with, observed, and interviewed people in many different kinds of organizations. It was as if we had put on a lens of hope. As the principles emerged, they were applied, tested and refined.

We believe more strongly than ever that the principles are true, deep, and transformative. The principles form the scaffolding of hope. They come to life in the workplace. They are practical, observable, and essential. In every story of real and resilient hope, one or more can be seen. When all five principles are present, they strengthen one another and set in motion a cycle of positive change.

1. **Possibility:** The search for opportunities in the face of obstacles

   This is where hope begins: with the belief that progress can always be achieved and that the status quo is never fixed or final. Possibility does not require false promises or sweeping visions; often it shows up as a quiet, persistent invitation to accept the idea that "things don't have to be this way." Leaders who foster possibility do not deny reality—they stretch it. They ask, "What if?" and "Why not?" and "What's next?"

INTRODUCTION

2. **Agency:** The capacity to act and influence outcomes

    Agency is the principle that reenergizes through action. No matter how tiny at the outset, some action can always be taken. Agency prefers contribution to keeping control. As a counter to inertia, an agentic person will say, "There is something here I can do that leads in the right direction." Leaders build agency by creating conditions in which others can act with purpose and confidence, making choices that count.

3. **Worth:** The sense that hoped-for outcomes have intrinsic value

    Hope depends on meaningful direction. If goals feel hollow or disconnected from civility and virtue, work becomes shallow or performative. When worth is present it often shows up as purpose, mission, or calling. "This work is hard—and worth doing." In organizations, worth can be a moral question: "Are we true to ourselves and one another?" "Are we serving a larger whole?" When people see a big picture imbued with fairness and generosity, hope thrives.

4. **Openness:** The willingness to stay receptive in the face of uncertainty

    Hope requires humility. It requires you to say: "I do not know, and I can learn." "I cannot control everything, and yet I can trust." "I expect to be surprised, and I can handle it." Openness requires resilience and flexibility. It embraces curiosity, dialogue, and adaptation. Real hope bends without breaking and sees options.

5. **Connection:** The experience of belonging with others in authentic relationships

When people feel seen, heard, and accompanied, and when "the truth" is welcomed, they are more likely to bring more of themselves to work. Connection is the relational foundation of hope: "We are in this together." It affirms that one person's effort matters more when it is part of a larger whole. In teams, connection builds trust. In systems, connection builds wholes greater than sums.

Why This Book? Why You? Why Now?

In the two decades since publication of *Putting Hope to Work*, you and we have experienced financial crises, political polarizations, deadly pandemics, ongoing wars, mass migrations, and climate upheavals. Events like these are not letting up. And, new since then, there is a revolution in artificial intelligence. The best leaders face a daunting mandate: Sustain momentum and meaningfulness in a context of disruption that seems beyond comprehension.

But to "make the case" for a new audience in a new context we needed to find out more about how success was being achieved in a heterogeneous range of hope-full organizations. We interviewed, worked with, and observed leaders in corporate, nonprofit, and educational contexts and heard their stories. Their examples are the source of our claims for the centrality of hope in today's world.

INTRODUCTION

We value hope in our private lives and personally know its relevance to how we show up in public, but this book belongs to a different category. Here we are focusing on what we know as organizational participant-observers: behaviors, activities, and outcomes in collective endeavors as they pertain to hope.

Our broad aim is to serve leaders of any stripe and calling, volunteers in charities, teachers in classrooms, executives in boardrooms, medical professionals in clinics, workers in teams, worshippers in congregations, citizens in communities, and influencers on social media platforms. You may not want to use the word "hope" in your communications under any circumstances—we know leaders in that camp. And yet we know, as one of our respondents remarked, "You don't have to be a firefighter to rescue someone from a fire." If you want a way to name what really matters, rally others toward new promises and possibilities and sustain shared momentum toward a desirable future, we are there for you.

In 2006, hope was a hard sell in managerial and professional circles. For the concrete operational crowd, hope was too soft and mushy—something nice to have, perhaps, but not related to a bottom line. In 2025, Gallup, a global polling and research organization, told a different tale. Gallup examined the needs of followers in 52 countries, representing 76 percent of the world's adult population and 86 percent of global gross domestic product. In their research, published as "What Do People Need Most from Leaders?" they asked a question and made a simple request:

1. What leader has the most positive influence on your daily life?

2. Now, please list three words that best describe what this person contributes to your life.

Here is their conclusion: "Hope is the primary need of followers worldwide, with more than half (56 percent) of all attributes linked to influential leaders pointing to hope—significantly more than trust (33 percent), the second most important need."

Among Gallup's findings these two points are most telling:

Workplace leaders hold tremendous potential to improve lives. Thirty-four percent of employed individuals cite someone from their work environment (manager, colleague or organizational leader) as most influential, just slightly fewer than those who name a family member (44 percent).

And with reference to the varied contexts of work, hope reduces suffering. When leaders meet followers' needs for hope, thriving is increased while suffering drops by one third.

Followers look to leaders for hope.

The Choice is Yours

Hope is an ally, not an algorithm. Hope promises capacity, not certainty. Hope takes it all in and acknowledges frustration and anger, skepticism and despair, while enabling joy, awe and love. With credit to the poet Walt Whitman, a defining voice of democracy: Hope is large, hope contains multitudes. Hope can embrace all of you, and all of us.

Hope at Work offers a field-tested, principle-based framework for building hope. Our hope for this book is that you will choose to become an agent of hope. Because hope at work makes a better future possible!

ONE
Choosing Hope

> "Hope is a decision. It is the most important decision we can make."
>
> Daisaku Ikeda, Buddhist philosopher and peacebuilder

An old Cherokee Indian was teaching his grandchildren about life. He said to them:

> A fight is going on inside me. It is a terrible fight, and it is between two wolves. One wolf represents fear, anger, envy, sorrow, regret, greed, arrogance, self-pity, guilt, resentment, inferiority, lies, false pride, superiority, ego, and unfaithfulness. The other wolf stands for joy, peace, love, hope, sharing, serenity, humility, kindness, forgiveness, benevolence, friendship, empathy, generosity, truth, compassion, and faithfulness. This same fight is going on inside you and inside every other person too.

They thought about it for a minute, and then one child asked his grandfather,

> Which wolf will win grandfather?

To which the old Cherokee simply replied, "The one you feed."

Hope is a conscious and intentional choice each of us can make at every challenging juncture. Life presents moments when we must choose hope, day by day, hour by hour, and minute by minute, always searching for a reason to move forward. Hope is also a choice an organization can make by baking it into the culture as a principle of leadership. This chapter is the story of a very large system choosing hope as a matter of course.

Embracing Hope as a Transformative Pillar of Culture

In the United States, Starbucks navigated Covid using hope as a leadership principle. Not wishful-thinking-hope, but pragmatic, muscular hope, informed by rigor, practices and principles. Hope that can be learned and practices that can be cultivated.

For context, the US represents 80 percent of Starbucks revenue. It is the heart of its business and culture. In 2020, there were twelve US regions, over 9,000 stores, 250,000 partners (employees), and 75 million customer connections per week.

Barbara's Note on Starbucks

To be fully transparent, I am not telling this story as a disinterested bystander. I was neither a bystander, not a disinterested person. When the pandemic arrived, I had been consulting with Starbucks on matters of culture for 20 years, through good times and bad. As a cultural anthropologist my role is Participant-Observer. I am "in it" while trying to keep a grip on my observing self. I would never have stayed with an organization for so many years without deep respect and affection for Starbucks' partners, mission, and culture.

I was privileged to work with and advise the US leadership team from eighteen months pre-Covid through Covid. I worked with hundreds of partners of all levels, functions, and geographies. Seeing the pandemic through their eyes was a front-row seat to every corner of the United States as we all dealt with a rogue wave of epic, life-or-death consequences. This is a case study of resilience, commitment, competence, caring, innovation, and hopeful leadership at all levels. Covid was a stark reminder that everything depends on how we choose to relate to uncertainty. All the "molecules" of the old ways of doing things were loose, swirling around, waiting to be reconfigured into new ways of being and working together. An opportunity for transformation. The US business chose hope over mere survival. Here is how they did it.

Background: Renewing a Foundation of Culture, Purpose and Hope, Pre-Covid

To understand the culture that was in place when Covid hit, it is important to understand the context. In 2018, Rossann Williams, a twelve-year partner who had been President of Starbucks Canada was named President of North American Retail. She faced a turnaround challenge. The United States had seen three leaders in four years. The business was under immense pressure, and the organization's spirit was fractured. Employees were operating in survival mode instead of striving for excellence. Wiliams said, "I will always be grateful for those twelve months before Covid. We gained clarity about who we were as individuals and as a team, which made us stronger when the storm hit."

The Twelve-Month Learning Journey

The following are a few of the key cultural practices that became a way of life pre-Covid, and a necessity during Covid. Leadership development was integrated with real work in a continuous learning cycle: questioning, fieldwork, meaning-making, alignment, and action. This dynamic approach was the lifeblood of decision-making and transformation. All quotes, except those otherwise identified, are from a wide variety of Starbucks leaders (see With Gratitude) who kindly gave us their time to reflect on the experience, two years later.

Habits of Hope
A. Hope as a Leadership Principle

From the beginning of Williams' tenure, hope was a central tenet of leadership, not a vague, wishful-thinking concept but a set of practical principals and behaviors. She said, "I wanted everyone to feel connected to the possibility that we can create a different reality." Leaders learned to discuss and embody hope, using the five principles to inform their culture-building. According to Williams, hope guided leaders to envision possibilities while staying grounded in the realities of daily operations: "Hope isn't just a warm blanket; it's a system—a disciplined way of thinking and leading. Hope doesn't excuse you from acting."

For hope to thrive, it must be rooted in truth. Leaders built trust by being transparent. As Thomas Friedman of *The New York Times* says: "Hope comes from seeing your leaders lead in a way that brings out the best in people by inspiring collaboration, common purpose, and future possibilities." Even in challenging times, truth-telling fosters hope. As Williams discovered, "Even when the news wasn't good, I learned that truth brings hope." One of our core tenants was, "When truth is spoken, hope enters the room."

A core principle was to employ a whole-system approach. As the late Marvin Weisbord, organizational scholar and co-founder of the Future Search Network, named this mantra, "Everybody improving whole systems." Holistic thinking and action were essential for Starbucks to thrive. Moving from siloed efforts to a unified community of purpose required intentional work across regions and functions, and between Seattle support and operations. Denise Nelsen, Senior Vice President of Operations, described the transformation:

> Previously Regional Vice Presidents focused on individual results rather than team success, which held us back. We needed to commit to the culture we aimed to build. We came together to define what success meant for all of us—not just individual regions. We created one team with agency. When the crisis hit, we were firing on all cylinders.

B. Honoring the Past — The Importance of Origin and Rituals

Stories of origin and rituals go back to the roots of our tribe. Not because they are "quaint," but because they speak to the essence of a community. And that is the connection to hope. As the writer Rebecca Solnit says, "Hope is grounded, but draws its energies from the past." Understanding our histories, victories, and complexities, is the foundation for envisioning a brighter future.

Attention to rituals was a key component of renewal. Rituals give meaning to our journeys, and a sense of purpose to our lives. They are critical to the health of the community, tribe, and family. Rituals afford a sense of belonging; they enact values, provide a sense of stability and continuity, and act as a bridge from past to future. Rituals enable us to access, honor, and strengthen our individual and collective identity.

Starbucks thrives on a rich culture of rituals, yet even the strongest traditions can wane in the rush of daily life. Restoring and renewing these rituals became a pivotal task. As one leader noted, "Rituals require sacredness and commitment. Building a culture of hope demands the same level of intentionality."

C. Fieldwork: Deep Listening and Observation

The real gift of using the field methods of cultural anthropology (ethnography) is that you get two things for the price of one. You learn what is "out there," while at the same time learning about what is "in here." Every organization, like each of us, carries its unique filters. For adults, direct experience is the most powerful practice we have for seeing the world with new eyes. We see things that challenge and surprise us. We begin to look *at* our lens—not just *through* it—opening the door to discovery and new possibilities for ourselves and places of work. These are the tools and skills that enable every team immersion to be as fruitful as possible, from inquiry, to analysis, to synthesis.

Adopting the mindset of an anthropologist, leaders learned to approach conversations with humble curiosity. Deep listening requires stepping out of comfort zones—away from the identity of problem-solver—and embracing the vulnerability that comes with discovery. Learning to "see with new eyes" requires being open to the surprise of having existing views challenged.

D. Context First — Creating a Rich, Shared Picture of Now

In a lecture, the poet Wendell Berry said, "Found your hope, then, on the ground under your feet." Hope is grounded in reality. Understanding our present context is the first step toward meaningful change. Shared context serves as a launchpad for hope-fueled action. Chan Hellman, founder of the Hope Research Institute, writes, "At the heart of change is our ability to understand the way things are right now in our lives, and then we can begin to imagine the way things could be. This is where hope is born." Creating this shared understanding requires leaders to foster spaces for meaningful dialogue, where multiple perspectives are heard, and collective meaning is formed.

E. Applying the Skills and Mindset of Organizational Learning

The field of organizational learning has given us the mindset and many of the practices that build a dynamic learning culture. These include framing the inquiry, inquiring and meaning-making through dialogue. Doing work in this way required leaders to bring a spirit of openness, vulnerability, and authenticity to team interactions.

F. Slowing Down and Convening Conversations

In our fast-paced world, slowing down is a radical act. It allows space for reflection, learning, and deep connection. "We needed a space to slow down, take a deep breath and summon a different energy." As Peter Block, a community-building thought leader writes, "When we gather in ways that awaken our collective possibility, we reclaim our power as a community." It requires a leader who makes and holds the space. Bringing people together for thoughtful conversations is essential. These gatherings prioritize inquiry—asking questions and exploring experiences—before leaping into solutions. It is in these dialogues that true understanding and meaningful systemic change emerge.

G. Storytelling

Stories are the lifeblood of culture. Telling stories can heal a community, while listening to them can build a community. They convey values, lessons, and shared experiences that data cannot communicate. Leaders at Starbucks embraced "story-stewardship," a concept championed by Brené Brown, the researcher and speaker, recognizing the profound impact of listening to and sharing stories. Stories were collected and shared on a regular basis by the leaders themselves. In times of crisis, it is tempting to focus solely on problems. While those stories were part of the equation, they were balanced with a practice that is rooted in Appreciative Inquiry, which challenges the tendency of leaders to give their attention to what is broken. Appreciative Inquiry invites us to look at what gives life to an organization, while a problem-solving orientation is centered on gaps and faults. Focusing on doing more of what works, the energy in the room shifts in a positive direction. Appreciative Inquiry highlights stories of hope and resilience without ignoring challenges. The journalist David Von Drehle writes: "The answer is not more crisis …, it is more time spent on the nurture of joy and cultivation of hope."

By 2020, Starbucks had achieved:

- A rebuilt and strengthened US leadership team and culture

- Improved same-store sales growth from low single digit to double digit in the first year

- Improved partner and customer engagement

February 2020: Enter Covid

> "Hope is being able to see that there is light despite all of the darkness."
>
> Archbishop Desmond Tutu, human rights activist

We know about VUCA: Volatility, Uncertainty, Complexity, and Ambiguity. And then there are Rogue Waves as described by Harry Hutson and Martha Johnson, former Administrator of the U.S. General Services Administration, in their book, *Navigating an Organizational Crisis: When Leadership Matters Most,* as archetypes for sudden, spontaneous, and significant organizational emergencies. "They come out of the blue, are fast-acting, unpredictable, uncontrollable, and consequential, implying life or death."

The Wave Hits: Choosing Hope During Covid

> "The signature of the truly great versus the merely successful is not the absence of difficulty, but the ability to prevail in the face of it."
>
> James Collins, author of *Good to Great: Why Some Companies Make the Leap ... and Others Don't*

It is hard to recall how quickly and drastically Covid changed our lives: silent cities, overflowing hospitals, deaths, and an economy in paralysis. An enemy we could not see; questions we could not answer. And then there were violent events leading to the global Black Lives Matter activist movement. At Starbucks, there was conscious effort to cope by balancing centralized decision-making with local needs. Operating in twelve regions with 250,000 partners, and 75 million customer connections per week, Starbucks was on the front lines. The response to Covid called for decisions with significant cost and indeed, life or death implications. Here are a few touchpoints in the Starbucks' Covid timeline recalled by Denise Nelsen that show the speed at which volatility, uncertainty, complexity and ambiguity ratcheted upward:

1. It started the week of 2/24. I was in Albuquerque visiting stores when we got the first call that someone was sick. We reinforced handwashing. Standing at the ABQ airport, I looked around and people were wearing masks.

2. I went on to Phoenix sitting in a store when the call came recommending people wear masks.

3. That weekend we got calls about more extreme next steps. We stayed very close to the science of it, learning as we went.

4. On March 2, we announced the closing of the Seattle Support Center.

5. Masks became mandatory the first week in March.

6. Around mid-March we shut all stores without drive-throughs (about 50 percent). A variety of policies were put in place for partners of closed stores. No one was laid off.

7. It was into the summer before shots were widely available.

8. We tried to re-open in May, then we had George Floyd and multiple closures in large cities.

9. Things became more normal by late summer but then there was another big outbreak around Thanksgiving causing closures. We used science-driven maps to make our decisions. If an area went over a certain level of infection we went to drive-through only.

Centralized decisions, even when informed by best available science, were fraught. To mask or not to mask? To require the Covid vaccine? How best to keep people safe? Every region of the country, and every store within every neighborhood had its own version of the Covid story: "We're in the same ocean, but in different boats." Regions, districts and stores, while complying with centralized decisions, needed extraordinary freedom and agency to make their own decisions. For example, in Texas, it became aggressively dangerous to wear a mask, so global decision-making required local mandates. It was a balancing act with high stakes, as described by Nelsen: "Despite the need for centralized decision-making during Covid, we worked hard to build one team that could navigate the universe of complexity and diverse needs."

Business Decisions that Fed Hope

"Hope is created moment by moment through our deliberate choice. It happens when we use our thoughts and feelings to temper our aversion to loss and actively pursue what is possible. When we choose hope, we define what matters to us most."

Shane Lopez, author of *Making Hope Happen : Create the Future You Want for Yourself and Others*

Decisions made during Covid clearly demonstrated that what mattered most to Starbucks was the health and wellbeing of its partners. Actions taken across the U.S. retail system included:

1. Allowing partners in the stores who were not comfortable or able to come to work, for any reason—which did not have to be proven—to stay home with their regular pay for more than a year.

2. Those who were able to work received additional "service pay."

3. At least quarterly (and often more frequently) a gift of gratitude and recognition went to all store partners, from t-shirts to pizzas.

4. In major cities with large groups of partners, Regional Vice-Presidents set up centers supplying basic needs from toilet paper to food.

5. The Workplace App was activated for store managers to increase access to each other and to leaders.

6. Nelsen held a weekly open forum for store partners that began with a coffee tasting and sharing of hope stories, followed by Q and A.

7. A virtual leadership development conference convened all District Managers to invest in their ability to lead through incredibly complex times.

In Nelsen's words, "We made the necessary technical decisions to keep people safe, and we leaned into investing in leadership and genuine care for others."

Cultural Practices That Fed Hope

Practices learned in the year preceding Covid, such as listening, storytelling, and dialogue, became essential. In times of crisis, leaders often default to command-and-control modes, discarding cultural habits built in calmer periods. But that was not the case in the US business. From Williams' perspective, "The investments we made in culture enabled us to thrive." Facing uncertainty, leadership mobilized at all levels, fostering unprecedented innovation in organizational process.

A. Slowing Down

> "The times are urgent. Let us slow down."
>
> Bayo Akomalafe, director of The Emergence Network

During Covid, Shannon Garcia was a Senior Vice President of the US Business:

> Before Covid hit, I was starting to see the power of slowing down and making meaning. The discipline to slow down. The discipline to understand the context. When everyone is running, running, running in every direction, what becomes really obvious is the power of slowing down to reflect and create shared meaning.
>
> It was the repeated slowing down, sharing stories, hearing each other's lived experiences and the experiences of those they

touched. It was the feeling of, "we're in a shared experience but it's different for each of us." It helped you grow, and it helped you feel that you weren't in this alone.

When Covid hit, I had only been at Starbucks for about two-and-a-half years, which meant I did not carry the deep history many of my colleagues did. But that also gave me a fresh perspective. One of the practices that stuck with me was gathering people in a room—not to rush into solutions, but to honor the past and the leaders who came before, and to surface the stories that shaped where we were. I remember thinking, "We're all standing in one room, but we're each seeing this system from different vantage points—different functions, years of service, even parts of the world." Slowing down to create that shared context wasn't just an exercise; it was a way of building hope.

I think about the months leading up to Covid as a kind of primer of how you build culture—creating connective tissue that allowed us as a system to define the future and create a collective sense of hope about what we were setting out to do. We were laying the groundwork for resilience. We didn't know it then, but that meaning-making would become our anchor.

But even in that darkness, I kept coming back to hope. We created spaces to slow down, even when it felt counterintuitive. Every week, we gathered—virtually—and shared what we were hearing, learning, and going through. It was raw, vulnerable and human. Executives aren't trained to say, "I don't know," but there we were, saying it out loud, together. And somehow, that made us stronger. It helped me not get sucked up into the brain of this is impossible.

I saw a system that had been so crystalized in how it worked turn into a vulnerable, open, willing-to-test-and-try learning system. I would never want this experience for anyone ever again, but it's such incredible insight around how to create. The system went from "I know all the ways and here let me show you how smart I am," to actually becoming a learning system. You didn't know. You had no idea. There was no playbook. There were no rules and the stakes couldn't have been higher. It energized so much hidden potential and creativity in the organization.

Hope is a choice, but it's not always easy to see. You need storytelling, shared context, or a simple moment of meaning-making to reveal it. And sometimes, you need someone to remind you of the autonomy and potential you already have. It's the moment you realize you're not a victim of circumstances.

Looking back, I realize how much this journey had impact on the person I am today. It taught me that even in the deepest despair, even when the future feels impossible, there's still potential waiting to be uncovered. Both things can be true: We can honor the pain, the loss, and the fear, while also choosing to see the hope and possibility ahead.

B. Psychological Safety and Shared Knowledge

"Sharing knowledge was essential. No one had all the answers. People were terrified, making life-and-death decisions. Our environment embraced authenticity and psychological safety—no one felt pressured to have all the answers. Everyone became part of a collective mind, figuring things out together."

Paul Pinto, executive coach at Starbucks

There was no master plan, but listening, reflecting, story-telling, and meaning-making remained priorities. Learning had to be dynamic and organic, addressing emerging issues in real time. The core belief remained: Systems contain their own best answers.

C. Storytelling and Story Sharing as a Cultural and Spiritual Anchor

"The first and last task of a leader is to keep hope alive. One way to do that is emphasizing hopeful stories. It takes four good things to overcome one bad."

Bill Taylor, a founder of *Fast Company Magazine*

Every conversation centered on storytelling—diverse narratives that grounded discussions in lived experiences. A ritual emerged: Every meeting began by sharing stories of hope. Some of these hope narratives were personal, others celebrated great moments in stores. They brought the light of possibility and agency into the digital "room." The stories were evidence of the hopefulness that lives among us, and they became an important way for leaders to keep their hope alive too. Everyone was a hope-carrier. While not negating or diminishing problems, partners took the time to stop and notice encouraging experiences. These living examples of hope were catalysts for transformation.

Nelsen dedicated leadership space and time for hopeful dialogue:

> What keeps coming up for me is that at a time when it was really complicated, everyone had things that gave them hope. They all had stories to tell and we almost didn't have enough time each week. There were so many lessons in seeing what was possible versus what was scary. And for me that showed through in big and small ways. We had to figure out as a team how to lead what seemed like endless changes for safety or when someone would have a personal loss or impact and the group would rally around them.

One partner called it "grounded hope." Leaders, knowing they might share, began actively seeking out stories of hope in their daily interactions. It is a truism that you get more of what you pay attention to. Small acts can have large effects.

Brady Brewer, Chief Marketing Officer, collected and shared customer stories of gratitude, describing them as a "reservoir of love and hope." He believed, "People go the extra mile when they know and believe in the why." He noted that although people now made more coffee at home, "They still came to our stores as a place to buy their favorite drink that can't be made at home and to feel a sense of connection or create an outing in the day to be around others."

Covid stories are more the little day-to-day interactions that are not specific to a person but rather examples of what we saw: partners rallying to create mask assembly lines; partners delivering free coffee to health care workers who were working crazy shifts; partners keeping their stores open to serve customers and their community even when there was danger in doing so; partners writing messages on customers' cups to help them feel connected to the world; partners being creative and resourceful and figuring out ways to operate their stores within the guidelines of the Center for Disease Control.

Crisis As a Transformative Opportunity: A Hopeful Approach

> "And in today already walks tomorrow."
>
> Samuel Taylor Coleridge, poet and philosopher

For the twelve US Regions, Nelsen embraced hope as a cultural pillar:

> We leaned into Covid with a focus on hope because it was foundational. We couldn't abandon our responsibilities, but we dedicated time to nurturing the culture we wanted. We embraced transformation as an opportunity—like entering a cocoon. We get to choose what kind of butterfly we come out as—we don't have to be the same. We can come out as something stronger and better.

The team was inspired by a butterfly metaphor from a scholar of hope, Rebecca Solnitt: "What Corona Virus Can Teach Us About Hope: In the Midst of Fear and Isolation, We Are Learning That Profound, Positive Change is Possible." When a caterpillar enters its chrysalis, it dissolves itself, quite literally, into liquid. In this state, what was a caterpillar and will be a butterfly is neither. It is a sort of living soup. Within this soup are the imaginal cells that will catalyze its transformation into winged maturity. May the best among us, the most visionary, the most inclusive, be the imaginal cells—for now we are in the soup. The outcome of disasters is not foreordained. In a conflict, when things frozen and locked up become fluid, there are both good and bad possibilities.

Culture is tested when times are turbulent. Having a clear and shared mission enabled the culture of the US business to thrive. Not only did the culture "hold strong," but I believe it strengthened. There is much to be said for having a clear mission.

Outcomes and Legacy

- Investments in culture and hope practices led to some of the highest store manager engagement scores (74 percent) and record low turnover at all levels of the retail business.

- Leaders emphasized aligning personal and organizational values, cultivating a sense of belonging and a purpose beyond profits.

From Nelsen's perspective, "Hope wasn't just about surviving—it was about building a culture that thrived and became self-sustaining, like an ecosystem of growth and resilience."

Hope is Chosen Not Given: One Leader's Story

There was no need to cascade hope practices. Leaders made them their own within their spheres of influence. When Covid emerged, Frances Ericson, a 27-year Starbucks' partner, was a vice president of the Pacific Northwest territory, approximately 600 stores and 14,000 partners. She took hope to heart, passing her learning on to her organization:

> Hope is something you can learn and it is an action. You must work at being hopeful and take personal responsibility for activating on it rather than being on the receiving end of someone giving you hope. It's not about being positive. Before

I used the language "I'm just a positive person," but really, I choose hope every day.

I think that the rigor we implemented in the calls and dialogue and homework—going out to listen and coming back together—taught all of us to be hopeful and create hope with others. It was a disciplined approach. The routine was life changing.

When the whole organization, specifically the retail leaders, started to focus on hope (and there was no hope anywhere else through Covid), we craved it more. If we hadn't focused on hope and we didn't learn how to create and foster it and lock arms together, Covid would have taken all of us out. We would have been wallowing in a corner in our home offices. We were starting to go into a dark place of helplessness, and we were able to turn from helplessness to, "We can do this."

Today, as I reflect on that journey, I know hope can and must be operationalized. It's not passive. No one can give it to you. It is something you can learn, something you work at, and something only you can choose. That choice, made collectively, changes everything.

The Lessons of Covid

Covid taught us many things. We learned that uncertainty is a way of life. We learned how interconnected and vulnerable we are. We learned that hope is something you must choose every day. Organizationally, the nimble learned to change and adapt at speeds even they were astonished by. In the face of personal and organizational exhaustion, we witnessed inspiring manifestations of resilience and creativity.

To varying degrees, organizations during Covid either blossomed with innovative ways of working, or they were sunk. At Starbucks, the US business experienced systemic collaboration only dreamed of in the past: new virtual networks, new possibilities for convening conversations, and new situational leadership springing up. Leadership emerged at all levels and evolved to meet the needs of the work within a framework of hope. The immune system was freed from self-imposed cultural constraints.

Culturally and personally, leaders benefited. They were released from old patterns. Necessity nurtured innovation. Confronted by something new and radically different, the system built resilience. The pandemic showed Starbucks what is possible. No one had the answers except for those that were discovered together. Every day brought new challenges for which there were no ready-made solutions. Being in the soup together encouraged risk-taking, rethinking, and rapid response. Covid taught Starbucks' US business how to learn and adapt together at "the speed of change."

This four-year slice of time is only one stretch on a long road marked by twists and turns. As a company in constant public view, Starbucks has weathered mishaps, struggles and repeated reinvention. Nelson sums up her experience:

> In a company like Starbucks, with over fifty years of history, you're bound to have highs and lows, good times and hard ones. That's the truth of any long journey. What I've learned is that who we really are shows up in our hardest moments. During Covid, when everything we knew felt uncertain, I saw something incredible. What could have been the worst of times became the best of times. People showed up for one

another. They led with heart. They found hope in small, everyday acts. That's when I realized, hope isn't an idea. It's alive. It comes to life when we create it together, one choice, one moment at a time.

Building Hopeful Futures

In the absence of an immediate life or death threat, the challenge for organizations is: Can we become more hopeful? Can we slow down enough to pay attention in life-giving ways? Followers want hope. Are we prepared to do the courageous and hard work of choosing hope?

A final reminder from Williams:

> I wouldn't want the reader to walk away thinking that practicing hope is simply for leading and evolving through crisis. We had started the work eighteen months previously to drive business performance, and the results were transformative. The pandemic just happened to interrupt the progress we were making pre-crisis.

Her words remind us that culture building and strengthening is ongoing work. Choosing hope is transformational in all kinds of weather.

Which wolf will win grandfather?

The old Cherokee simply replied, 'The one you feed.'"

TWO

Hope's Rewards

"People flourish when they feel hope in their neighborhood and in their bones."

Lionel Tiger, anthropologist

In 1995, we published our first article addressing hope in organizations, "In the Company of Hope." We were seeking to understand hope collective hope and to lean away from fear. It felt like new territory because research in organizational health rested on models rooted in the "3 Ds": disease, deficit, and dysfunction. The first scientific wake-up call had been sounded in 1959, at the annual meeting of The American Psychiatric Association. Karl Menninger, M.D., winner of the Presidential Medal of Freedom, presented his colleagues with this challenge:

> Our shelves hold many books now on the place of faith in science and psychiatry ... but when it comes to hope, our shelves are bare. The journals are silent. Are we not duty bound to speak up as a science, not about a new rocket or a new fuel or

a new gas, but about this ancient but rediscovered truth, the validity of Hope in human development.

Hope Pioneers

In social psychology, the study of individual hope was pursued by C. Rick Snyder and his team in the Hope Research Group at the University of Kansas. Their "hope theory" has become a mainstay. Hope was defined as a sense of successful agency (goal-directed energy) and pathways (planning to meet goals). Sometimes known as Will-Power and Way-Power.

Snyder's Hope Scale is a proven way to understand "high hope" individuals, for whom hope does the following:

- helps academic performance
- increases athletic performance
- contributes to physical health
- contributes to psychological health
- assists in the achievement of goals
- encourages connection

Harvard Medical School professor, Jerome Groopman, M.D., has explored the role of hope in health and healing. In his *The Anatomy of Hope: How People Prevail in the Face of Illness*, from 2003, he posited "an authentic biology of hope." According to Groopman, belief and expectation are key elements of hope, releasing endorphins and enkephalins in the brain that act to block pain, and unleashing a "domino effect, a chain reaction in which each link makes improvement more likely. It changes us profoundly in spirit and body."

Richard Davidson, who founded the Center for Healthy Minds at The University of Wisconsin-Madison, investigates the neural bases of emotion and human flourishing. In a conversation with the Dalai Lama in 1992, he was asked, "Why have you been using the tools of modern neuroscience to study anxiety, fear, and depression? Why not use these same tools to study kindness and compassion?" Davidson's lab has since explored well-being, joy, resilience, and happiness.

Discoveries in modern medical science have helped us understand more of the details of how well-being is embodied. Well-being is not an ephemeral psychological state or condition but is very much intertwined with our organ systems in ways that have consequences for our health.

In 1998, a survey of 30 years of psychological publications counted 46,000 papers on depression, and 400 on joy. Martin Seligman, president of the American Psychological Association, said, "Social science now finds itself in almost total darkness about the qualities that make life most worth living." Seligman promoted the new field of positive psychology in the 1990s, whose focus is hope, optimism, resilience, courage, gratitude, and perseverance. Positive psychology has since taken hold. It is now common to describe and appreciate what is healthy and what is good, what is adaptive and what is working, in individual and collective behavior. The result is a more balanced and nuanced picture of both disease and health, deficit and abundance, dysfunction and well-being

Hope Research

We can truly speak of a "science of hope" through many within many disciplinary frameworks. Data support the impact of hope on individuals, on organizations—and on brains. A few highlights illustrate that hope is just plain good for us.

Shane Lopez, a Gallup Senior Scientist, writing in *Making Hope Happen: Create the Future You Want for Yourself and Others*, connected the data points of hope research and concluded that hope is a driver for many of life's most desired behaviors and outcomes, including:

- Boosting Well-Being: Hope spurs us to pursue what matters most. This gives us a greater sense of control and purpose, keys to well-being and resilience.

- Enjoying Good Health: How we think about the future affects our health.

- Living Longer: Hopelessness predicts mortality. Hope is a proven boost to medical aids.

A 2025 study by Megan Edwards and Laura King at The University of Missouri analyzed responses from over 2,300 participants across six studies and found that hope, on its own, reliably enhances peoples' sense of life's meaning. Their findings, published in the journal *Emotion*, challenges traditional views of hope as merely goal-oriented and reframes it as a cornerstone of psychological health. Their work demonstrates that hope, more than happiness or gratitude, fosters the sense of meaning crucial for overall psychological functioning, better relationships, and improved physical health.

A summary of the impact of hope on us as individuals touches all spheres of our lives. At the top of that list are:

1. Psychological Well-Being: Hope is strongly correlated with higher life satisfaction, lower levels of anxiety, depression, and stress. Hope fosters resilience by helping individuals cope with adversity, trauma, and uncertainty. Studies in positive

psychology suggest that hopeful individuals have better emotional regulation and greater optimism about the future.

2. Cognitive and Decision-Making Benefits: Hope enhances problem-solving abilities by encouraging people to focus on solutions rather than obstacles. It is associated with greater goal setting and motivation, leading to persistence in the face of challenges. Research in cognitive psychology shows that hopeful people exhibit more adaptive thinking patterns, making them less prone to learned helplessness.

3. Health and Medical Outcomes: Patients with higher hope levels experience better recovery rates from illnesses and surgeries. Hope is linked to improved immune function and reduced inflammation. Studies on chronic diseases suggest that hope contributes to better pain management, longer survival rates, and improved quality of life.

4. Cellular Impact: What about the things we cannot see? Social science research on hope has been complemented by neuroscience research on the physiological impact of hope on our brains. Recent neuroscience findings emphasize that hope is an active cognitive process deeply rooted in specific brain functions and chemistry. Hope activates brain regions involved in planning, motivation, and emotional regulation, specifically the prefrontal cortex, essential for goal-directed behaviors, and the orbitofrontal cortex which helps reduce anxiety and improve problem-solving.

5. Neurochemistry of Motivation and Mood: Hopeful thinking triggers the release of key neurotransmitters. Dopamine activates the brain's reward and motivational circuits, providing the drive to pursue goals and find meaning in life. Serotonin is involved in mood regulation and positive emotions, helping individuals maintain a hopeful outlook during adversity. Norepinephrine contributes to feelings of motivation and arousal when facing challenges.

6. Protective and Resilient Effects: Studies in 2024 show that hope acts as a protective buffer against stress, anxiety, and depression. Individuals with high levels of hope tend to view obstacles as manageable challenges rather than insurmountable threats; bounce back more quickly from setbacks; experience less emotional turmoil and lower stress hormone (cortisol) levels; have better physical health outcomes, including a lower risk of heart problems.

7. Neuroplasticity and Rewiring: Consistently engaging in hopeful thinking can lead to long-term structural and functional changes in the brain via neuroplasticity, strengthening neural pathways associated with positive emotions and resilience.

Findings at the cellular level reinforce and help us understand hope's psychological impact. Brains "on hope" show distinctive patterns: stronger communication between sensory/motor parts and the cerebellum (which is involved in coordinating action). That suggests hope is reflected in how the planning, sensing, and doing parts of our brain are integrated.

In plain language, hope rewires us. Hope helps us feel better and prepares us to do things.

Organizational Impact

Our research in the years before 2006 yielded recognition by the editors of *Harvard Business Review*, who summarized our work as "The Leader from Hope" and recognized it as a "breakthrough idea for 2007." In recent *HBR* articles, hope is framed as a measurable and trainable leadership capacity that drives resilience, engagement, innovation, and ultimately better bottom-line performance. Here are three examples:

"The Strategic Power of Hope" (December 4, 2024)

> Stanford Professor Jamil Zaki, author of *Hope for Cynics: The Surprising Science of Human Goodness*, explained that hope is not just optimism or wishful thinking, but a dynamic combination of willpower (motivation to achieve goals) and waypower (finding pathways to achieve them). It counters negativity bias at work, enabling leaders and organizations to see opportunities and act creatively amid uncertainty. Hope fosters resilience, engagement, and innovation, ultimately contributing to measurable organizational success and adaptability.
>
> Hope acts as a bulwark against self-defeating behavior and narrows focus from problems to possibilities. Leveraged properly, it can drive organizations to thrive even in turbulent conditions.

"Sustaining Hope in Uncertain Times" (March 15, 2022)

> Dane Jensen, a CEO and business school faculty-member at Queen's University in Canada, discussed the essential role of hope for motivation, health, and performance during crises such as the pandemic. He framed hope as a difficult but vital self-management skill that balances acceptance of uncertainty with belief in a better future. The piece underscores hope as foundational for endurance and organizational recovery.
>
> When hope is lost, so is our will to endure and ultimately prevail. Hope requires accepting that we cannot know the future while believing things will improve.

"Research: The Complicated Role of Hope in the Workplace" (October 18, 2022)

> Management professors Katina Sawyer at the University of Arizona and Judy Clair at Boston College reported research findings on how hope interacts with workplace emotions during ambitious or challenging projects. They present hope as intertwined with both collective and individual experiences, influencing motivation and team morale, especially during setbacks and celebrations. Their advice: Embrace both the "highs" and "lows" of hoping but avoid unrealistic expectations.
>
> Hope emerges in contexts where employees face uncertainty or are working towards challenging goals, and shapes their motivation and shared emotional experience positively.

Research that tests the efficacy of hope at work continues to compound. Recent findings connect hope to bottom-line results and provide empirical support for the argument that hope is both a motivational ideal and a strategic resource that enhances performance, engagement, and profitability. For leaders focused on credibility and results, these findings are backed by rigorous, peer-reviewed studies involving thousands of employees.

Meta-analyses and systematic reviews of research conclude that employees who feel hopeful perform better, engage more deeply, and generate more creative ideas. This conclusion comes out of contemporary work published in professional journals such as *Psychology* and *The Journal of Positive Psychology*. Hopeful employees are adept at setting goals, identifying multiple pathways to success, and adapting to obstacles—qualities that directly contribute to superior outcomes and organizational resilience. One large-scale study covering more than 1,000 employees across 135 organizations demonstrated that hope, alongside optimism and resilience, is significantly related to enhanced job satisfaction, higher organizational commitment, and stronger work performance.

These studies are not limited to self-reported feelings. Research includes supervisor ratings, employee performance assessments, and organizational indicators that skeptics and results-oriented leaders will recognize as credible measures of business impact. We predict that studies will continue to show that hope will be positively correlated with job satisfaction, employee retention, and work engagement.

In today's context of disconnection and "quiet quitting," Lopez' findings regarding the workplace impact of hope are telling:

> Showing Up: No other workplace or school metric counted more than hope in determining whether employees or students showed up.

Being Productive: Times of uncertainty and complexity require higher hope cultures that display perseverance, collaboration, and enhanced problem-solving ability. Hope predicted higher performance at all levels of employment and education.

With a strong scientific foundation, we can summarize the findings. Organizations that cultivate a culture of hope see higher engagement, satisfaction and productivity. Hopeful leaders inspire greater innovation, risk-taking, and long-term strategic thinking. Teams with higher collective hope have better collaboration, resilience, and adaptability in moments of challenge.

The Biggest Reward of All

Jane Goodall, at age 90, viewed hope through the longest lens of all: evolution. In *The Book of Hope: A Survival Guide for Trying Times* she writes:

> We are going through dark times...
>
> Hope is often misunderstood. People tend to think that it is simply passive wishful thinking: I hope something will happen but I'm not going to do anything about it. This is indeed the opposite of real hope, which requires action and engagement...
>
> Hope is contagious. Your actions will inspire others...
>
> Let me say that without hope, all is lost. It is a crucial survival trait that has sustained our species from the time of our Stone Age ancestors.

Her words lead to the conclusion that matters most for leaders. We are not lost. The evidence for hope's impact is clear and compelling. The work ahead is to enlarge our awareness, develop actionable concepts, and apply grounded practices to cultivate hope at work.

THREE
Create Possibility

> "Nothing is impossible, the word itself says 'I'm possible'!"
>
> Audrey Hepburn, actor and humanitarian

Hope is born in possibility, which is the first of the five principles we identified in our research years ago. When we began to incorporate the "power of possibility" into our consulting practice and became better accustomed working in-between—in between what our clients considered impossible to achieve and what they understood to be inevitable—we witnessed the achievement of welcomed and unexpected results.

The word possibility comes from the Latin root *posse*, meaning to be able, to be powerful, to be feasible. It is related to the word potential, the capacity for growth and development. By cultivating possibility-driven thinking, you do more than dream—you shape a future where hope is a lived reality. Consider that the principle of possibility underlies every breakthrough, revolution and positive transformation in history.

We understand there are barriers to possibility in organizations, not least is the need to meet or exceed stakeholders' expectations. Under-promise and over-deliver! Consider how easily the voice of possibility can be drowned by "realists" (and cynics): "We can't do that without more resources." "That's never even been tried." "There's nothing to see here—let's move on." So, play it safe. Pick your battle. Stay inside your circle of control. Everyone has a favorite temporizer and ideation-killer. It is easy is to play this game—and it feels natural. But the opportunity costs of the human tendency to default to criticizing ideas and stifling imagination are real: "We never saw it coming!" is a lame (or tragic?) response in a watershed moment when a crisis occurs or when fortune escapes.

McKinsey, the management consulting firm, concluded from a survey of more than a thousand companies around the world that "the ability to innovate" is the most important strategic factor for generating growth soon. And what does their research say about how to do this? Leaders must foster an aspirational mindset.

An aspirational mindset and a possibility mindset are similar in that they both focus on growth and achievement, but they have key differences in focus and approach. Whereas an aspirational mindset focuses on long-term goals, ambitions, and personal growth, often requiring planning, discipline, and persistence, it can also lead to frustration when the gap between where you are and where you want to be feels too large. A possibility-way-of-thinking, in our view, is a cultural umbrella. Under it, you see opportunities and you embrace curiosity, creativity, and adaptability. Possibility encourages exploration and enables flexibility and persistence even when events do not unfold as planned.

In our original set of interviews, a leader remarked that the "mindset of possibility is powerful day and night in terms of innovation, and it multiplies chances of success by an order of magnitude."

No doubt, each of hope's five principles, taken alone, is exposed and fragile. Possibility-thinking, as a sustainable practice at work, requires full-fledged hope. There needs to be agency—doing something and not just predicting whether something can or will happen. Possibility also relies on having a purpose to achieve positive ends—the principle of worth. There must be courage, alertness, and stamina—key dimensions of openness. And teamwork is required for meaning and momentum, which is the principle of connection. When hope is alive, and all five principles are enacted and interwoven, the combined effect lifts each principle and creates an effect more resilient and powerful than the sum. Our intention in this chapter is to retain the inherent simplicity of the principle of possibility while illuminating how possibility can be applied at work to generate enthusiasm and achieve aims.

Possibility is Born in Curiosity

As Senior Staff Researcher at Google, Jay Hasbrouck, a social anthropologist, combines ethnographic and foresight methods to identify what drives change and to mine for strategic opportunities. Hasbrouck's goal is to pique the curiosity of his clients in a way that enables them "to entertain new possibilities." His thinking is ancient: "It is impossible for a man to learn what he thinks he already knows," said Epictetus, the Greek Stoic philosopher.

Hasbrouck says, "I don't know that you could be curious without having some hope. Applying a curious mindset increases the odds that new ideas will inspire our work." He writes of both the evolutionary and neurological value of curiosity to humans and other living species, in terms of adaptation, survival, and surprise: "Neurologically, experience suggests there's actually a neural link between surprise, memory, and the drive to learn more."

If curiosity is necessary for us evolutionarily, why are there such varying degrees of curiosity observable in organizations? A clue is the presence of anxiety, one of the great inhibitors of organizational curiosity. The more pressure there is to come up with the right answer as soon as possible, the less curious people become. The range of possible outcomes shrinks as people tend to avoid discovery and surprise by staying in the known world.

Music producer Rick Rubin, in *The Creative Process: Reflections on Invention in the Arts and Sciences*, says that living in discovery is always preferable to living in assumptions. Truer than ever in today's volatile and rapidly changing environment, where assumptions narrow the path to learning, shutting down "the ability to entertain new possibilities." Another limit on curiosity may be the lack of humility in organizational culture. If leadership values having all the answers, chances are good most people march to that drumbeat.

Staying truly curious requires staying grounded in humility and being open to learning. It requires leaders who have an appetite for discovery and who are willing to be surprised. Leaders who are teachable. Chris Argyris, one of the founding fathers of organizational learning theory, in "Teaching Smart People How to Learn," said humility is the necessary starting point for learning. Humility leads to curiosity. Curiosity leads to discovery. Discovery leads to growth.

John Winsor, a thought leader on the future of work and co-author of *Open Talent: Leveraging the Global Workforce to Solve Your Biggest Challenges*, writes:

> In times of great change, the most resilient leaders are the most curious ones. We are living through one of the most profound transformations in the history of business. Artificial intelligence is no longer a distant vision—it's here, now, reshaping

how organizations operate, how employees engage, and how customers experience value.

Leaders may feel overwhelmed by the pace of change. But one truth remains constant: Curiosity is your most powerful mindset.

Ignore Culture—at the Expense of Hope

Jon Francis is Chief Data and Analytics Officer at General Motors. Francis comes from a world of numbers. His education is in mathematics and statistics. For much of his career, he believed that the key to making decisions was simple: "I always thought you only needed data—behavioral data in ones and zeroes—to make decisions."

When Francis first stepped into his role at GM, the mindset was clear: Data are for counting. "We know how many cars we're making, how many we forecast, how many batteries we produce, and so on." The company has an engineering mentality from top-to-bottom and uses data to measure what has already happened. Francis sensed data could reveal something far more valuable—what was possible. When the market research department was merged into his organization, he thought he needed more data scientists to handle the load, but the move sparked his curiosity. He began to realize that combining ones and zeroes—with talking to people—could create a powerful narrative to redirect practice and be more customer centric. To do this, he hired a qualitative researcher.

Francis now sees his purpose as something much bigger than analytics: to be a cultural change agent, someone who fosters curiosity, learning and empowerment within "an amazing and iconic company" that has been around since 1908.

The core challenge that I'm seeing is that there are all these siloed sources of information supporting specific business units. How do we create a more holistic picture and a company that says we don't want to be product-led anymore, we have an aspiration to be consumer-centric, and let customers tell us where they want to go and what products and services and capabilities they want from us?

Francis determined that GM needed stories—first-hand accounts from real people—to make the data come alive. GM needed to listen more to customers. What did that mean in practice? It meant shining a light on possibility by asking what signals are hidden in their vast collection of data that can show a new direction?

We were going from the very engineering mindset about the role of data and counting widgets to, how do we interrogate data in a different way and tell stories around it? How do we create insights? There's no better source for that than talking to customers.

One of the biggest struggles is breaking the habit of relying on the "hippo"—the highest-paid person's opinion. Too often, decisions are made based on rank, experience, and instinct rather than what customers are saying. When one of the company's first EVs rolled off the lot with high expectations, customers began experiencing feature bugs.

Francis and his team gathered data from multiple sources—customer service calls, behavioral patterns, engineering reports—and connected the dots. "We put together a one-pager that laid out the problems using stories, insights, and behavioral data. When we showed it to senior leadership, their minds were blown. They appreciated the hypothesis backed by qualitative and quantitative data." That is when he knew: This is how to drive change.

> As I started to get leading technical resources, I realized that this stuff is really hard in a way I had never anticipated. It doesn't matter how damn good the analytics are or how you present it, how much revenue it's driving or how much cost could be cut from the P&L. I tried a lot of different techniques on how you present materials and how you think it through, but I realized it was never about the analytics itself, which is kind of crazy. It was about the culture.

What keeps him going? Continued transformation with a focus on customers and more human-centered approaches.

> For me it's about how we build the culture at GM, at the crusty old age of 115, to where everyone truly feels empowered, not just to make decisions but also to fail—and it's going to be okay, and we'll even be better for it.

He thinks about this transformation every day. "If I find myself banging my head against the wall, maybe I'll know the organism is rejecting me. But building phases are never easy, and we're tasked with building greatness at this iconic American company, which is incredibly motivating." In a follow-up conversation with Francis, he was very hopeful:

> I'm inspired by the culture work we're doing. It has been more amplified than when we spoke, including defining new

behaviors for the company and really pausing to reflect, to say, well, what got us here?

Part of the behavior work has been acknowledgment and recognition that there're some things that we need to continue to honor that have made GM special and that you wouldn't want to lose.

But then there are certain behaviors that we're going to double down on that will be different and hard for the company. I'm on this task force sponsored by the highest levels of leadership at GM.

The culture piece is probably more important than ever because there are just more headwinds: global trade and economics, competitive pressure, EV adoption. It's a challenging environment, but it also creates opportunities.

Overall, I'm still very hopeful, thanks in part to how our senior leadership team views the importance of culture to drive our business performance.

At this point in the story Harry observed, "It strikes me that in an engineering culture like GM, if you want to ground behaviors in leadership work, you better darn well be grounded in data."

How will we know it's helpful and additive? We talk a lot about measurement and linking behaviors and culture from a statistical perspective back to business performance.

> My goal is to be recognized as a leader who drives change in a way that honors the culture and brings people along.

Take Action to Unlock Possibility

The wisdom of leaders: "Possibility for the sake of possibility is a trap. Dreaming is not moving the enterprise forward." In our words, get moving so more can happen. "If you open yourself to possibility," we were told, "it's more likely to occur, and you make your own luck." According to Byung-Chul Han, a philosopher of hope whose thinking is grounded in pragmatic possibility as the route to profound change, "Hope opens up for us a field of possibilities. Only then can we set our eyes on a concrete goal."

When the principle of possibility is fully hopping (*hop* is a root of hope), forward movement can come in leaps or, according to John Winsor, in small steps.

He posits that the key to adaptation in a digital world is shifting to a more distributed idea of an organization that revolves around talent (people) and projects, not divisions and offices. In this "networked organization," talent is culled from both inside and outside, in a global ecosystem that can be tapped as needed. "We're standing in a moment where new models are replacing old. Much of our work can be done better by machines. What now is our place in the world?" This is the very question many find themselves asking in the face of disruption, uncertainty, and loss. "The ground is moving beneath us. We are in a shift as big as the transition from the agricultural to the industrial age. Organizations and mindsets have been structured around outdated models, and now AI is accelerating this change. It's terrifying." Winsor echoes Jon Francis at GM:

Work has been structured in the industrial age to be productive in putting nuts on bolts in a car factory. That's kind of the "Henry Ford" way that in which we've all been programmed. Organizations are structured that way. People's mindsets are structured that way. They were built in an analog age and don't have the required flexibility in the new world of digital work that's only going to get accelerated with AI.

For Winsor, the way forward includes creating a new paradigm—perhaps an "open talent economy"—where companies can access a "crowd" of skilled individuals beyond traditional employment boundaries, including freelancers, consultants, and independent contractors, to tap into diverse expertise on an as-needed basis. Companies can scale their workforce up or down based on project demands. Open talent platforms allow companies to find talent from anywhere in the world. If that is the future of work, big changes in skills and attitudes are in store: "What I find really interesting is that we, as humans, are adaptive to this future organization."

Winsor thinks about global and generational trends in the world of work, including "the Pandora's Box" of artificial intelligence. "Hope is essential, and we need more hope now than ever." But before a new paradigm of work can take hold, according to him, we have to say goodbye—and grieve the loss of—our old mental models. This is personal work, intimate work: small steps everyone needs to take. In turbulent times like these, Winsor believes they lead to hope. When he recently taught an executive seminar with hundreds of senior leaders from around the world, participants talked about not just organizational renewal, but personal renewal. Winsor realized that the first step of renewal is acknowledging emerging circumstances and new conditions.

When we talked with Winsor a year later, he said, "What I love is that no matter where you are in the world, we all have access to the same experts. What I think about is the power of individual agency—the power of having the information without being weighed down by bureaucracy." Winsor contrasted today's abundance with the world of 25 years ago: "These weird organizational hierarchies that came from a world of scarcity, where you waited as long as necessary to see 'the expert.'"

> We used to go to school to get knowledge, and now we can find out anything, anytime, immediately. So what should we be teaching kids? Should we be teaching them how to have better human relations, build better community, figure out how to ask the right questions?

From his perch looking at the future of work, Winsor could not be more hopeful:

> The deeper I dive into this, the more fired up I am about the future of work and how open talent democratization is transforming organizations. By embracing diverse voices and perspectives, companies are supercharging innovation, adaptability, and creativity like never before.

Create Possibility

In their book *Tomorrowmind: Thriving at Work with Resilience, Creativity, and Connection—Now and in an Uncertain Future,* Gabriella Rosen Kellerman and Martin Seligman emphasize the critical role of creativity in today's rapidly evolving work environment. They argue that while our ancestral hunter-gatherer brains are naturally inclined toward creativity, a trait essential for foraging and survival, modern work structures have often stifled this innate ability. The authors assert that, despite the challenges posed by automation and technological advancements, human creativity remains a unique asset that cannot be replicated by machines. Their conclusion rests on what Jon Francis and John Winsor describe as the post-industrial narrative: Creativity and innovation are "our uniquely human gift, restored to workplace prominence today after its assembly-line decline." As Peter Drucker said, "The best way to predict the future is to create it."

Steven Tepper is a nationally recognized leader in creativity and education who was appointed president of Hamilton College in 2024. Previously at Arizona State University where he was dean and director of the Herberger Institute for Design and the Arts, Tepper became known for combining the disciplines of art, science, engineering, technology, and media while cultivating an inclusive learning environment and promoting interdisciplinary collaboration. For Tepper, a transforming education for today's world requires making creativity and human expression central to learning, discovery, and civic engagement.

Tepper represents both old (he wears bow ties) and new (his youthful energy and enthusiasm are to behold). For Hamilton College, this means rethinking the role of creativity in education. Historically, high value in this venerable college of liberal arts has been placed on analytical skills. Tepper argues that we need to cultivate creativity with the same intensity. "We don't get a four-year degree in hope," he jokes, "but we do in creative practice."

Hope and creativity are two words that seem inseparable but, as Tepper explains, have distinct roles in shaping our world. "Hope requires the consideration of alternatives and of future possibilities that might be different from the present," he told us. Creativity, on the other hand, is "a practice, a discipline," something that requires rigor, repetition, and refinement. The two are interconnected, but they are not the same. Hope enables creativity, and creativity fuels hope. Tepper explained that creativity means expanding possibilities beyond perceived limitations: "Any creator is counting on designing something unconstrained by current conventions, capacities, and conditions that may be in the way of human flourishing."

For years, we the authors have experimented with teams and creative exercises—for example, building "organizational sculptures" out of toy figures, tinker toys, alphabet blocks, clay, yarn, and found objects—and they have always come out the other end, maybe slightly disoriented at first, and then feeling hopeful. Tepper told us, "I would definitely say creative practices should generate hope." In our experience, creative learning activities yield enthusiasm, insight, emotional engagement, and even fun! Creativity also generates energy and momentum.

When I was at Arizona State University," Tepper told us, I hired a woman, Liz Lerman, who's a distinguished choreographer, MacArthur Genius Grant winner, a very wise person with amazing things to say about hope." Lerman often spoke about the difference between shape and momentum in dance. "Shape is an essential dimension to consider, but what's equally important is the momentum that gets you from one shape to another.

For Tepper, this analogy applies not just to dance but to institutions like Hamilton College. "A lot of the strategy for an institution like Hamilton is to try to give people a sense of momentum. Because I think momentum puts you in a different space. It breeds hope. You're starting to feel a forward motion and energy, that something is possible here, that things can change positively and productively."

Momentum, "unsticks people from those conventions and assumptions that don't allow them to move forward. It makes the naysayers less effective because it's easier to shoot at an object that's stationary than one that's moving." Rather than waiting for perfect clarity, he builds forward movement through action. "Even if you don't know exactly where you're going, I think you should build strategies for momentum."

From a designer's perspective, Tepper suggests using "a lot of prototypes and pilots—things that you don't have to spend four years debating and voting on, but you can just try." He describes this process as "extend them, reinvent them, but get things moving."

Early successes are also essential. "I think early wins are part of creating momentum," he explains. "We think about particles in a solid state as not moving. But if you start to heat them up a little bit, they can start to form other formations. Our faculty, staff, and students may not even know what other formations they could take, but by introducing small movements, a little positive heat, you generate early motion."

Tepper stresses the importance of recognizing critical junctures. "I think it's really important for people to recognize and to feel a sense that we have reached a moment where there are inflection points." He believes this recognition creates a sense of possibility. "The world has given us an opportunity here. We need to decide if we're going to take it."

For Hamilton College, Tepper sees this as a defining moment. "This is a unique moment in time for this institution, given its environment, given what the world needs, given our assets. We need to step up to the plate." He emphasizes that defining the moment is crucial. "People have to understand it, and it has to be authentic. They have to say, 'Yes, this is Hamilton's moment.'"

Tepper links this idea of momentum to Hamilton's historical roots. "We were founded and named for the most creative founding father, who was a builder of possibility, of institutions, of ideas." The challenge now is whether institutions and individuals will seize this moment to shape the future. Momentum, possibility, and hope are not abstract ideals; they are created through action—a theme we recognize. "You don't always know what shape you'll take," Tepper says, "but by getting things moving, by creating motion, you open the door to transformation and hope."

What If?

At his inauguration, Tepper introduced the "What If?" initiative: a platform designed to foster creativity, interdisciplinary collaboration, and innovation within the campus community. This initiative encourages students, faculty, and staff to propose and develop transformative ideas that can reshape the educational landscape and enhance the college's commitment to the liberal arts. What If invites members of the Hamilton community to ponder ambitious questions that challenge conventional thinking. Examples include:

- What if we had a way to engage meaningfully with artistic expression and environmental sustainability?

- What if we used AI to create new forms of educational content to engage our students?

- What if we activated our public spaces differently to create a more inclusive campus?

By framing inquiries such as these, What If aims to transform speculative ideas into tangible projects that embody the creative spirit of a liberal arts education. It seeks to connect islands of thought and practice, promote cross-disciplinary collaboration, and foster a culture of experimentation and inclusivity.

The Hamilton community has come alive. Inauguration events featured academic presentations where faculty and students collaboratively explored What If scenarios, exemplifying the initiative's collaborative ethos. Additionally, the groundbreaking of the Innovation Center in the fall underscored the college's dedication to fostering an environment conducive to creative exploration and interdisciplinary learning. Three tiers of proposal funding are now available to accommodate a range of project scopes:

a. Spark Propositions: small-scale ideas

b. Catalyst Propositions: more complex projects involving broader community partnerships, spanning up to an academic year for development

c. Transformational Propositions: ambitious initiatives aiming for significant institutional impact and long-term transformation

In parallel with funded projects, What If is sparking creativity in faculty teaching. Learning to cope in disruptive environments requires novel teaching strategies. Here are three examples:

- Kevin Grant, a professor of history, relies on the concept of instability to invoke creativity. He inserts spaces into courses and conversations, whereby students might turn in new directions. He asks questions where he does not have answers. Creativity happens when "the students and the instructor are in it together with no specific end in sight."

- Dean and professor of creative writing, Tina May Hall, builds in constraints to her writing exercises such as setting a timer for 90 seconds and then asking for a written piece with one-syllable words, then changing it up and asking for an anecdote written about your grandmother's hairbrush, then the thing that saved you from a fire, and so on. "The key is to momentarily break our normal patterns and allow our thoughts to get strange, to go to unexpected places, to find the cracks that suddenly widen into beautiful expanses that feel like freedom."

- Steven Wu, a professor of economics, encourages students to be mindful of small details in their environment that could lead to research ideas. For example, combining locality with an issue of global importance, he might ask about how living in a rural community might impact the well-being of refugees in the nearby city of Utica, NY.

"Let's try things," says Tepper. "Let's start experimenting, prototyping, piloting. We do not have to wait. The future is now. Let's begin."

For Tepper, as for Hamilton, there is also the importance of honor. As a cornerstone to the institution's identity, there is an Honor Code that emphasizes the institution's commitment to academic integrity and ethical conduct. The Honor Code is not merely a formal policy but a precept that imbues the culture with mutual trust—and emotional regard. "If hope implies change and change implies loss," Tepper asks, "how do you help a community move, and how do you honor those losses?"

Being highly aware of possible futures for academia, Tepper wonders, "How do you honor people who have dedicated their entire lives to being really good at a certain thing, even if the future might require a different thing?" He says that in any organization, especially if you're hoping to change, everybody, should feel honored.

Tepper bolsters the importance of taking small steps by providing an example of a small act of kindness:

> It doesn't take a lot to write a letter to a classicist who may not be driving enrollments anymore, or may not be using the most advanced technology and otherwise getting awards, but about whom a student said to me, "I love that class with this faculty member," and I send them a personal note saying I talked to a student today who said, "Your class is the best class, and I know how much you dedicate yourself to teaching, and you are making a difference." Like that. Takes me three minutes.
>
> That classics professor might have been the harshest critic, or the person who is resisting change and is angry and feels like the new computer science building is taking resources away from their department. But they're going to feel a little differently knowing that they are still seen, and they are still valued, and they are still honored.

Hamilton's direction is mirrored outside academia. National Science Foundation research shows that welcoming creativity and integrating arts-based learning into professional environments can enhance overall organizational performance. By engaging in artistic activities, leaders develop better communication skills and teamwork abilities, essential for effective leadership and collective success.

Steven Tepper admires Bill Friday, president at the University of North Carolina for 30 years, who was widely respected for integrity, leadership, and dedication to public service. Friday was known as a "merchant of the spirit" for his belief that universities should do more than provide technical knowledge: They should uplift hearts and minds by shaping the character, values, and civic responsibility of the community. With Tepper at the helm at Hamilton, Friday's inspirational leadership has found a new home.

Two Indicators

We know when possibility is present, and when hope is building momentum, by paying attention to two indicators. Consider these two points as the distillation of our message, intended for groups at work.

A. Passion

We often say possibility is a "passion for the possible," in Kierkegaard's phrase—the relentless pursuit of what could be, the belief that new realities can be created, and the commitment to transforming potential into actualization. Possibility inspires you and generates energy, and you can feel it!

B. Pragmatism

Hope applies when future events are neither guaranteed nor are they out of reach. The sweet spot of possibility is setting goals with the right amount of stretch. Then, with possibility in your wheelhouse, you put one foot in front of the other and you get moving!

In 2004, Paul Rogat Loeb, activist and scholar known for his work on social justice, activism, and civic engagement, edited *The Impossible Will Take a While: A Citizen's Guide to Hope and Fear*, a collection of more than 49 fragments, stories, and essays by extraordinary leaders and writers about how ordinary people can make a difference in the world through grassroots activism and community involvement. Nelson Mandela, Marge Piercy, Vaclav Havel, John Lewis, Alice Walker, Martin Luther King, Marion Wright Edelman, and many others. Loeb captured the essence of our chapter in writing, "Possibility is the oxygen upon which hope thrives."

FOUR
Activate Agency

"Hope can flourish only when you believe that what you do can make a difference, that your actions can bring a future different from the present."

Jerome Groopman, M.D., author of *The Anatomy of Hope: How People Prevail in the Face of Illness*

Agency is hope's springboard. Hope unleashes action, and action generates hope. It is a generative cycle that builds momentum and delivers goodness. Agency is the belief that our actions make a difference. Having an element of control over one's future enhances hope. As people act and see progress, hope grows, creating a positive cycle of motivation and engagement. With agency, hope becomes a motivating force for change. Exercising agency is choosing to be involved and to participate fully in the moment.

In this chapter our focus is on a single story of how agency can deliver hope and healing in a hospital and the communities it serves.

With respect for and gratitude to the Eastern Cherokee Nation, we focus on the Cherokee Indian Hospital in North Carolina and its remarkable, agentic, and hopeful leader, Casey Cooper.

Hope is a Call to Action

The Eastern Band of Cherokee Indians is a sovereign nation with more than 15,000 enrolled members. Their home is the 56,600-acre Qualla Boundary located in five Western North Carolina counties. Their hospital is the Cherokee Indian Hospital Authority (CIHA). Cherokees have always held true to their robust values and deeply rooted principles: Group Harmony; Spirituality; Strong Individual Character; Sense of Place; Honoring Our Past; Educating Children; Sense of Humor.

Casey Cooper is the first and only CEO of the Cherokee Indian Hospital Authority in Cherokee, North Carolina. He led the effort to achieve self-determination for the Cherokee Health System from the US government—which came to fruition in 2003. Cooper was the catalyst, from conducting the initial feasibility study to leading the system from start-up to healthcare showcase. He has been its head for over a decade. By taking control of their healthcare system, the Cherokee people reclaimed autonomy over their well-being and future.

Cooper is a modest and self-effacing man who pays attention to you when you speak and then listens carefully. When he speaks, others listen respectfully and intently. In an interaction with Cooper, there is a felt sense of wisdom being imparted. He is also a natural storyteller.

Cooper gave us the gift of inviting us into his culture and sharing his tribe's way of seeing and understanding the world, especially the realm of healing. Looking through the lens of hope at work, we see the principles enacted everywhere. Cooper says,

When I was a child, I remember experiencing a kind of fatalism. There was widespread poverty. There was a lot of abuse and neglect, and there was no access to community capital. It wasn't until we had this huge economic revolution [with the introduction of legalized gambling] that started in the 1990's that we started to see possibilities. Without resources, it's hard to have hope.

Newfound economic opportunity in "the blessing that presented itself" allowed the community to reimagine what was possible. With resources came the ability to dream of a healthier, more self-sufficient future, and to make those dreams a reality.

The Seed of Transformation: A Mission Beyond Profit

Although the tribal health system is funded solely from revenues made possible by a major casino investment, it is non-profit.

> One of the things that's unique and different here, partly a strategic and intentional choice and partly a blessing, was being a tribal health system.

> There's not a lot of ambiguity around our mission—to reduce health disparities and elevate the health of the local community. In essence, that's what we do here. We don't exist for profits; we don't exist for market share. We exist to ensure there is an Eastern Band into perpetuity. So, our core purpose is very different from other health systems. Our core purpose is to ensure the prosperity of the next seven generations of the tribe.

Grounded in shared ownership, self-determination extended from the system to the individual. As a community, the tribe stepped into full responsibility for their healthcare system. Tribal agency was enacted in building trusting relationships with patients and motivating them to pursue their own healthcare. Organizations use many words for agency: empowerment, ownership, engagement, which signal both personal and collective capacity to act.

Jerome Groopman espouses "the overwhelming medicinal value of hope." Cooper practices what Groopman teaches. "A true physician not only treats the disease but teaches the patient how to strengthen their own sense of agency in the healing process." When we asked Cooper about his biggest challenge he said, "overcoming fatalism." Global economist and well-being expert, Carol Graham, writes,

> Lack of hope is a vicious cycle undermining agency. Those who have hope believe they can overcome problems and seek support and help in doing so, while those who do not are more doubtful of the future, less trusting of others, less likely to seek help. Restoring hope requires reducing uncertainty, restoring self-confidence, agency, and trust in others.

Under Cooper's guidance, the CIHA addresses the whole person and the person's ecosystem. Agency is baked into the patient experience. Starting with the premise of shared ownership: "This belongs to you."

The Primary Care Team: Nexus of Healing

Providing patients a cross-disciplinary, team-based approach is the basis for holistic solutions. Cooper explained how the healthcare system is designed around integration with the primary care team:

We constantly cultivate culture that understands that the rest of us exist to support the influential relationship between patients and their primary care team. It doesn't matter that we're competent, or that we practice evidence-based medicine. What matters is the ability to build an influential relationship that motivates you to be engaged in your own healthcare—including basic diagnostic tests..

Right Way Training

At the heart of Cooper's story is relationship—right relationship, deep and meaningful connection.

The most important thing I can tell you is that we have a training that we do pretty much every other month. We call it Right Way training. In the Cherokee language that means asking, "Is the individual on the right path in life, living right?"

We are teaching people the nuts and bolts of effective communication: dialogic practice, advocacy and inquiry, relationship building. We're also teaching the importance of being safe and vulnerable. You have to be safe with vulnerability to authentically participate in perspective-taking which is the essence of empathy.

This training takes three days. Our goal for this year is to finish up with 75 percent of our staff. We've been on a journey to have a high degree of saturation. It's essential to our culture, so that when our employees leave that training and go back into the workforce, we're creating an ecosystem of people who have common values and skills, and who understand the expectations for building therapeutic influential relationships.

Imparting hope to others has nothing to do with exhorting or cheering them on," writes Parker Palmer, teacher, writer, and activist. "It has everything to do with relationships that honor the soul, encourage the heart, inspire the mind, quicken the step, and heal the wounds we suffer along the way."

Sharing and Receiving Story

Commitment to action begins with voice—having a voice in discovering and planning the future, being the change versus being changed. Voice is to be included, to matter, to be seen and to have a say in the future. In the words of Tommy Orange, a member of the Cheyenne and Arapaho Tribes of Oklahoma and a creative writing teacher at Institute of American Indian Arts MFA program in New Mexico, "It's just as important for you to hear yourself speak your stories as it is for others to hear you speak them."

Learning to share and receive stories honors and strengthens voice. It has been said that, "We are listened into voice." Giving someone a voice is a gift of agency. Medicine's most fundamental act, according to Groopman, is not prescribing a drug or ordering a test, but listening to a patient's story. In our consulting work, we teach people how to share story and how to receive story in a healthy way. In order to be influential with you, then I have to be able to accept your story. I have to have a genuine interest in your story. For me to have genuine empathy and compassion for you, then I need to understand what an honor it is to hear your story.

When we are "listened into voice," we are much more likely to take an active part in shaping the future. We are no longer mere bystanders. When we are listened into voice we feel a sense of personal ownership. Cooper says, "We teach people these things to understand how essential it is to live in a way that is comfortable with being vulnerable and authentic and genuine." This embodied storytelling is tangible evidence of agency.

> We endeavor to be recovery-friendly. If you ask me, why are we putting so much emphasis on hiring people in recovery? I do it because of hope.

> We do it because this community needs to see a person who is two years into her sobriety, who is just radiant and beautiful and glowing again, like the Creator intended her to be.

> We endeavor to hire every single person who wants to work here, maintaining their sobriety, because they are a constant illustration of hope. That is the epitome of transcending fatalism.

Calling in the Elders

Elders are the voice of the culture. They bring the gift of perspective. The practice of honoring the wisdom of elders is a story of survival, renewal and resilience. In the words of Stephen Charleston, Native American elder and retired Episcopal bishop of Alaska, "Elders are not a quaint relic of the past, but a living source of strength for the present. Elders are a people of the future. They have survived many struggles and losses. Elders have a passion for tomorrow." Elders give voice to the long threads of the culture, making the connections from past to present to future. They provide the cultural glue and continuity that is a foundational source of strength for any people, tribe, organization, or family. Elders can see and hear through the noise. By providing the perspective of having come through hard times, they both preserve culture and pass on a sense of collective and personal agency.

Cooper spoke of the system's early days, giving words to Mission, Values and Vision.

> We were trying to get clarity about who we are and why we exist. It was almost an academic exercise at first. We would put these phrases on the wall and debate a word for hours. We kept saying, "Are we losing something in translation? What if we're really not getting to the essence of what our customers think is most important?"
>
> In the absence of culture, all that strategy stuff didn't matter, so that's where we needed to focus. So I was able to get a group of volunteer elders who were also fluent speakers.

The elders' insights shaped the organization's vision, reminding the community of the importance of sustaining the soul of the tribe by remembering its deepest values.

> I would bring them together a couple of times a week for a month or so. And I would feed them lunch, and we would sit in a small conference room with dry-erase paint on the walls. We had all these phrases on the walls, and we would just talk. And they would say, "Tell me what you're getting at with that mission or value," and we would tweak the words.

Eventually, I said, "Is there something we're missing here?" And that's where the Four Guiding Principles came from. They said, "This doesn't really work for me. They're just there for the paycheck. They're not given from the heart." And that's where it was. We adopted them as the standard of behavior in the healthcare system.

Cultivating culture here is getting people not only aware of our Guiding Principles but actually feeling and living them every day.

Cherokee Guiding Principles for Hope

- Guiding Principle One: The one who helps you from the heart. "This community doesn't care what you know until it knows you care."

- Guiding Principle Two: A state of peace and balance. Cherokees believe that all things strive to achieve this ultimate state of peace—where everything is in balance as it should be—can only be achieved through healthy relationships and is fundamental to living healthy lives.

- Guiding Principle Three: It belongs to you. CIHA believes that all healthcare services belong to the people. The Eastern Band of Cherokee Indians Tribal Option acts as a steward of this inheritance, ensuring healthcare is safeguarded and provided to patients and members when and how they need it.

- Guiding Principle Four: Like family to me. CIHA is committed to being the healthcare partner of choice for this community, reinforcing the relationships found in healthy families.

By re-grounding Cooper's team in their four guiding principles, the elders are living reminders of what matters: the attributes that have provided sustenance and resilience for millennia. They are the bedrock of agency.

Incorporating Indigenous Practices and Values

Honoring key cultural practices and values by incorporating them into the very lifeblood of healing practices assures a continuity of cultural identity and agency during transformation. "What matters is whether we build an influential relationship," Casey knows, "and part of that relationship incorporates older ways, older ways of knowing, older ways of healing, older belief systems, older rituals."

> My Aunt Dora was experiencing the early stages of renal failure. As a young nurse I was really perplexed by the desire she had to withdraw from treatment therapy and just stay home.
>
> Why would she stay home when she had access to the latest technology? I assumed it was because she was uninformed about what was in her best interest. It wasn't until later that I discovered it was actually peace in her last years that she desired. It wasn't longevity. It was peace. And to be at home where there was love and beneficial relationships.
>
> And that became one of the services we offer here: hospice suites to honor and acknowledge what an important part of life this is to families. When we bring those folks home and

love on them, we support families and the communion they have.

Deeply rooted habits that underpin culture are, for good reason, the most difficult to change. This was Cooper's insight on his journey from being naïve nurse, thinking problems could be solved through technology and education, to savvy leader. He realized the "right way" forward lay in integrating the best of both worlds—building on rituals and not competing with them. It is a practice that honors Indigenous wisdom and traditional ways, assuring elders that they have voice and influence. Its respectfulness builds agency and pride by affirming that the past informs the future.

The lesson here for change agents is not to rush to transform or start something new without thinking it through. We stand on the shoulders of our ancestors, and there are lessons to be learned.

Indicators of Success: Signs of Hope at Work

Byung-Chul Han writes that hope is a spring with a determination to act. What keeps agency alive is achieving results. We asked Cooper how he knew the healthcare model was working—both through measurable outcomes like patient health improvements and system efficiency, and through less tangible but deeply felt shifts in culture, trust, and community well-being. By the numbers:

Employer of Choice:
1. Grown from 125 to 900 employees
2. Turnover rates consistently lower than healthcare benchmarks
3. Employee engagement scores above 80 percent

Provider of Choice:
1. Many chronic disease measures above the top quartile and some top decile compared to benchmarks
2. Most customer satisfaction scores in the top quartile

Investment of Choice:
1. In partnership with NC Department of Health and Human Services, the first Medicaid Indian Managed Care Entity in the country
2. More than $250 million in capital for construction of new facilities and a substantial annual appropriation for service expansion and enhanced benefits, all provided by the Eastern Band of the Cherokee Indians
3. Annual operating budget increased from $26 million to more than $180 million annually
4. Cash reserves of more than 500 days cash on hand

By the Heart

Cooper told us that the most important thing is to be significant in the lives of people we care for. "How would I know?"

1. When we bring a patient "home" to a hospice suite, surround them with love, empathy and compassion, replacing pain with memories ("Really miss momma but your staff made it possible"), we're treating emotional pain with positive memories.
2. We have significance over multiple generations. People come in scared and anxious. They've just had a new diagnosis, and we're alongside them. When people call my cell, It's a cry for help. We get to be there, sit with them in the pain of new information.

3. When a family hugs me in the grocery store.
4. We know we are a significant source of pride for the community. When tribal leadership entertains dignitaries and they show them the health system.
5. We are significant in mitigating stress through our patients' access to common capital: a $400 million infrastructure. They are the owner. They are proud.
6. I know from patient testimonials that restate our corporate values. It's significant that we are the provider of choice because of relationships and trust. And we get the psychological benefits of pouring ourselves into others. To hear someone say, "They treated me like I was family."

There are no more important indicators than these.

Agency Fuels Action and Action Fuels Agency

Agency begets hope which begets agency in a positive cycle that begins with acting. Action builds self-confidence and self-efficacy, which nurture hope, encouraging us to become increasingly proactive in creating the future. This is the generative spiral of agency. As confidence builds, dreams become bigger and more ambitious. As we move from bystander to participant-owner, our sense of possibility expands. Where once we may have perceived barriers, we now see challenges and learning opportunities.

The principle of agency unleashes not only our hope, but also our commitment and willingness to think creatively and work toward goals we really care about. Hope activates agency, which in turn, creates more hope. As Brené Brown writes, "Hope is ... believing that your voice and actions matter."

Organizationally, agency is our willing involvement and participation in a collective endeavor. When we feel truly agentic, we turn ourselves from passive observers to active participants. The shift is from noticing what needs doing to stepping in and doing it. Our mental, physical, and spiritual energy is most engaged when we are included in planning and making decisions about issues that affect us. When people are left out, they may go along—but without the energy that comes from having shaped the outcome. Alexander Hamilton's observation that "Men often oppose a thing because they have no agency in planning it" applies to everyone! The power of delegation, co-creation, and distributed ownership is self-evident to hopeful leaders.

Agency requires adequate resources, as Cooper explains. It is hard to have hope when there are too few resources to get the job done, and efforts are starved.

Agency often requires the courage to act into the unknown; the courage to advocate for an innovative idea; the courage to speak the truth of one's experience; the courage to make a difference. In "Doing the Hard Work of Hope," the consultant and author Annie McKee writing in the *Harvard Business Review*, says "Hope is nothing without creative action. Hope is not passive. It's active and calls for energy and courage."

The Meaning of Hope for Casey Cooper

For Cooper, "Hope is the prosperity of the next seven generations. Hope is transcending all the horrible things that adversely affect communities that are structurally disadvantaged."

Within the Cherokee Health system, hope and core purpose are one. Cooper's story casts hope as intention put into practice—not waiting and wishing. Cooper's leadership establishes hope for the ages. It is a deliberate act of building a future that honors the past, serves the present, and benefits descendants. Healing has many sources, and hope heals in many ways.

FIVE
Uphold Worth

"Far and away the best prize that life offers is the chance to work hard at work worth doing."

Theodore Roosevelt, statesman, naturalist and warrior

Work worth doing, the essential element for hope to grow and flourish in organizational settings, gives hope its "why"—its meaning and purpose. Hope fuels our will to survive, our longing to belong and our commitment to work together. Hope, as an expectation for a better future, realistic engagement in the present, and awareness of strengths drawn from the past, is a defining force in human life.

Psychiatrist and author Robert Coles, who spent years caring for seriously ill children, once told a story of a twelve-year old polio-stricken girl immobilized in an iron lung, hopeful to her core, who told him, "I may not get there with my steps, but I'll leap there with my mind."

For Coles, the child revealed a reality about the basic makeup of people: "Hope is the defining aspect of our humanity, not only as an emotion, or state of mind, but something, again, that goes to the very heart of our nature: a biological expression of our insistence that we last as a species, and as individuals who belong to it."

Survival, after all, is worth at its most essential, a primary source of personal and collective agency. In this chapter we present how this works. We suggest that individual dignity and collective prosperity are interdependent and mutually reinforcing. And we show how choosing to align with worth, personally, professionally, and organizationally, is a smart move.

Not Giving In

When Harry lived in North Carolina, he made a point of meeting the late John Hope Franklin in Durham when he was 90 years old. "John Hope," as he was called by many who knew him, was an historian, activist, grandson of an enslaved man who fought for the Union, winner of the Presidential Medal of Freedom and more than 100 honorary degrees.

On a beautiful spring day, Franklin was delighted to show off his greenhouse where he raised over 100 varieties of orchids—including four named for him. In his kitchen, he told Harry a story from his childhood that bears retelling. His story illustrates the power of personal and family values.

Franklin was born in Rentiesville, Oklahoma, near Tulsa, one of 50 Black towns established by African Americans in Oklahoma before 1920. There were thirteen Black towns remaining in 2025. The population of Rentiesville is 91. (Harry had taken a pilgrimage there when he lived in Oklahoma and discovered that the Franklin house is now an empty lot.) Both of Franklin's parents were formally educated. His father was a civil rights lawyer who defended survivors of the 1921 Tulsa race massacre.

One day, when he was six years old, John Hope and his mother flagged a moving train to take a trip. When they found empty seats the conductor told them, "You can't sit there." The conductor stopped the train and put them off in the woods.

He was crying, but his mother admonished him: "That's nothing to cry about. The conductor was enforcing the law. Blacks and Whites are not supposed to sit together. Don't you waste your time. Use your time to prove you're as good as anyone else on this train."

And that is what he did. In his words, he "rose above sentimentality"—although he admitted his middle name gave him a "bright outlook," at least "subliminally."

As David Dodson, a philanthropy educator and past president of a foundation in Durham observes, parental messages like what Franklin's mother delivered were essential to survival in the Jim Crow era. Hers was a version of "The Talk," a critical conversation that Black parents have with their children, particularly sons, about navigating racial realities in America.

Franklin left Oklahoma to attend Fisk University, earned a Ph.D. at Harvard and taught at seven colleges and universities. Always a kind and generous person, he gave "unstintingly of himself" to colleagues and students of all backgrounds. As an activist, Franklin believed in an "untrammeled democracy"—a high bar at this moment of writing. John Hope Franklin believed in himself, and in hope.

Gallup can help explain Franklin's remarkable journey. Their CliftonStrengths framework, with 25 million assessments in its database, identifies 34 human "talents" (talents become strengths when they are put to work), and Belief is the one that causes people to be "family-oriented, altruistic, even spiritual, and to value responsibility and high ethics."

Belief-oriented individuals are characterized by their unwavering commitment to act on their values. Belief is consistently described as having "core values that are unchanging." Belief talents are described as "a wellspring of powerful drive and direction."

Hope requires the belief that something of worth is at stake, and that:

- The self is worthy of imagining a better future,
- The goal is worthy of pursuit, and
- The effort is worthy of action.

Worth inspires us to defend our values and resist the unwelcome or the wrong.

The story of Rosa Parks, who lived a life of steadfast moral convictions, is another example of the power of having worthwhile values and beliefs under the weight of Jim Crow laws. In 1955, in Montgomery, Alabama, Rosa Parks had refused to give up her bus seat to a White person, not because she thought she would succeed in changing the culture and system of segregation, but because she believed in the fundamental dignity and equality of all people. She later said, "People always say that I didn't give up my seat because I was tired, but that isn't true. I was not tired physically … I was not old … I was tired of giving in."

Parks knew she would face arrest, harassment, and threats. She had no guarantee her actions would lead to change. Parks was aware that she might "be manhandled but I was willing to take the chance … I suppose when you live this experience … getting arrested doesn't seem so bad."

Her actions sparked a bus boycott that led to a national movement—at great personal cost to her and her family. She was soon fired from her department store job, and her husband Raymond, also politically active, was fired as well. They never found steady work in

Montgomery again and were forced to move to Detroit. She endured decades of health and economic trouble while remaining steadfast as a Civil Rights activist.

Parks acted based on her certainty that segregation was wrong and human dignity was worth defending. Her stand was not calculated for success; it emerged from her core values and belief in what was right, regardless of the consequences. Parks lived for 92 years. Near the end she wrote, "I try to keep hope alive, but that's not always the easiest thing to do."

On a drugstore bag found in her belongings, she had written, repeatedly, "The Struggle Continues."

Time for Worth

Aron Ain, long-serving and now retired CEO of Kronos, the company known for computerized time clocks, is a multi-year recipient of awards from Glassdoor as Highest Rated CEO. He is also author of the acclaimed *Work Inspired: How to Build an Organization Where Everyone Loves to Work*. David Solomon, CEO of Goldman Sachs, offered this blurb: "Aron Ain's book shows why building an authentic company culture is as important to long-term success as any other business decision." We surmised Ain knew something about hope.

When we spoke with him, Ain admitted he is not prone to use the word "hope," although he sees himself as a hopeful person. "I always try to create an environment where people have hope and, and they feel like there's an opportunity for the future to be brighter than today ... a better place, a better world, a better society."

Hope was evident in his core beliefs, however: trust, truth-telling, accountability for doing one's best, challenging and innovating, allowing flex schedules (long before Covid), welcoming back prodigal employees, empowering the next-generation workforce, and more. It is a long list of worthiness. Ain guided us to see how the principle of worth was central for him and core to his leadership philosophy and practices.

First, there is hope's inherent relationship to new beginnings and possibilities. Ain's principled leadership is evident in his early advocacy for working parents, particularly mothers. In the 1980s, when flexible work arrangements were rare, Ain pioneered policies allowing employees to work from home or maintain part-time schedules.

His progressive stance was not merely a business decision—it was deeply personal, influenced by his mother's experience as a Columbia Law School graduate who had to choose between her legal career and raising her family. "My mom would have had a very successful career, but she didn't have the opportunity in the world that she came from, where corporate America didn't support or embrace the idea of working moms." The story of Ain's mother—graduating from law school at nineteen, passing the bar before she could practice, and later returning to law at age 50 after having raised five children—became a catalyst for his commitment to creating more inclusive workplace policies.

> We had these fantastic young women who worked for us. I was a young man at the time myself. And it typically happened when they had their second child within two to three years, they said, "It's too much; I can't do both"
>
> I said, "Whoa, slow. I need you to stay. You're too good. You've invested too much; we've invested too much."
>
> Then I asked, "What would it take?"
>
> They said, "Well, can I work from home?"
>
> Done.

This personal history transformed into a corporate mission to ensure that talented professionals would not face the stark choices his mother encountered. Was Ain being pragmatic? Yes. Inclusive? Yes. Principled? Yes again.

A second and crucial dimension linking worth to hope lies in its power to motivate moral and ethical agency. This is evident in how Ain approached trust as a foundational principle: choosing to trust employees from the start rather than requiring them to earn it. It is codified in the company policy of unlimited vacation time.

> I believe trust is the magic glue that holds together personal and professional relationships. Trust belongs to the person who extends it. I can't insist or demand that you trust me. I own my trust, and I give my trust to people to whom I want to extend it.

Ain begins all relationships personally and professionally by trusting people. When he would observe managers interacting with new employees in an untrusting manner, he would call them to account and ask, "Did you hire them? Did you interview them? When you were interviewing them, did you say to yourself, they're really good, but I really don't trust them? I assume you trusted them when you were going through the process. So why don't you trust them now?" In this simple yet profound way Ain instilled his belief in the worth of a principle that empowers people. Ain continued:

> And maybe hope is in that same category. I can't make someone be hopeful. But maybe we can create an environment that we allow people to have hope and be hopeful.

Third, worth's connection to hope is cemented through its orientation toward collective benefit rather than individual gain. Ain said:

> We're a better company because we're more diverse. We're a better company because we're more inclusive. We're a better company because we fight hard to make sure that people can find a home and feel like they belong. And I think it's good for business and it's always good when things that are good for business, also are the right thing to do.

The creation of Employee Resource Groups (ERGs) at Kronos generates outcomes that benefit the broader community. There are now ERGs for the Jewish community, the Islamic community, veterans, people with cancer, and more. Before there were any disability laws, Ain reduced barriers by doing simple things like installing automatic front doors. And most important, he reduced barriers by meeting people.

> We had 16,000 people. On a site visit, I would say hi to every single person I saw and shake their hand and ask them how they were, how their families were, and what they were working on. It took maybe 30 to 45 seconds for each conversation. That was a form of communication for me, just telling them I cared about them. I wanted to personally greet them because I knew it was important.

After several live interactions with Ain, Harry can vouch for these behaviors. There is always a warm greeting and handshake, a look in the eye, a personal question that registers as authentic. It is easy to see him walking hallways and factory floors as the same person everywhere he goes.

When the open vacation policy was instituted at Kronos—which codified employee trust—engagement scores skyrocketed, turnover plummeted, and business results were the best ever.

For Ain, it was part of his job to teach in Kronos' leadership program Courage to Lead. For him the action word in the title was "courage," not "lead." It takes courage, he said, "to be a great leader who can have difficult conversations." Exercising courage is an act of "caring kindness." He adds courage to his two mainstay values of communication and trust.

When worth is understood as hope's deepest core, hope-filled leadership, as exemplified by Aron Ain, gravitates toward practices that recognize human dignity, empower ethical action, and generate widespread positive impact. Ain told us, "I never really thought about my work is giving people hope, by trusting them and communicating with them." What could be simpler?

Hope in Haiti

In our interviews and research, we consistently find that people and organizations who foster hope are those who align their efforts with causes greater than themselves. Worthwhile goals—creating jobs, serving customers and communities, building skills, providing safety and meaning—become rallying points that unlock human resilience and imagination.

We heard stories about self-help in Haiti—about reforestation and women's health that personified how worthy aims can generate hope—not just in corporate America. In Haiti, a legacy of foreign intervention, political instability, and natural disasters seems never-ending. At this writing, Haiti is experiencing a catastrophic humanitarian crisis driven by gang violence that has displaced a 1.3 million people. Civilians are caught in the crossfire. Haiti has devolved from what was once the richest colony in the hemisphere to its poorest nation.

We learned, however, that well-directed institutional and individual efforts performed by Haitians themselves, sometimes assisted in the right ways by dedicated outsiders, can put life into hope—and indeed, hope into life. Worth showed up both in motivating concrete steps and in inspiring positive outlooks. We have seen this dynamic play out repeatedly. And too, we have learned how the process of pursuing worthwhile activities has had positive ramifications for individual people, for local groups, for the economy, and for health.

Michael Anello, a former child psychologist who is now the head of a reforestation project as well as a family health system in Haiti, is our source. After decades as a psychologist, Anello experienced a profound loss following the suicidal death of a young client. It "rocked his world." Needing a change in direction, Anello wound down his practice and was soon looking for something else to do when a friend prompted by the 2010 earthquake in Haiti suggested they go there to help in some way. This was a calling and the start of a new career.

Anello was drawn to what he found in the wake of the earthquake: people who had lost loved ones and whose homes had been destroyed—people with "absolutely nothing"—being happier than many people back home in the U.S. Anello's volunteer trips over the following two years transformed him as a helping professional. Knowing nothing about construction, he was nevertheless asked by a foundation to be an in-country construction manager. He was able to recruit and manage workers, and while receiving technical advice from an engineer in the U.S., he created a workforce that built a church.

He remembers "walking up the hill to this church and being overwhelmed that 25 Haitians and I, who could barely communicate with each other, were able to do this together, and it became the center of this little community." Next came a school, houses, and a health center, and eventually Anello became a program manager for two initiatives—reforestation and women's health—another shift in his career. Both, worthy efforts in themselves, soon benefited from Anello's holistic approach aimed at sustaining local communities.

Hope's Seeds

To reverse Haiti's long history of deforestation, CODEP or Comprehensive Development Program, a Haitian organization, has chosen to focus on improving watersheds by planting almost 18 million trees over 35 years. The CODEP Way is a strict and consistent regimen for preparing soil, performing nursery work, planting on the mountains, and maintain long-term care. As a result, reforestation efforts are sustained across generations—in contrast to shooting seeded mudballs out of airplanes, which is practiced by other reforestation efforts. COPEP's slogan is that "it takes five years to plant a tree," which emphasizes how critical are the nurture and protection of new plantings—and the protection of the soil itself. It is also true that eucalyptus trees are so big in five years that they are not easily cut down and hauled away by just one person.

In his role as director of a reforestation partnership working with CODEP, Anello has learned what is required for sustainability at the local level: incentives for farmers to plant and grow trees—and defend them from thieves or goats—markets for fruit, jobs for youth, natural fertilizers, measures to prevent erosion, education to build environmental awareness, basic healthcare, and food for those who cannot afford it. These factors combine and coalesce to create an ecosystem in a community. This is worth as a systemic practice.

To seed hope in Haiti, Anello began a mentorship program for young people in 2020 that combined classwork on sustainable living with practical experience in planting trees. By planting seeds gathered from rotted fruits at the markets, there could soon be mangoes, oranges, and avocadoes for people who could not afford to buy food. "I figured out that if I gave young people something to do, it would give them the desire to continue, and it would give them a job, and it would give them hope for the future of their community." Several of the young men and women who graduated have since become university-trained agronomists.

One quiet young man, whom we will call Ford, demonstrated remarkable initiative and leadership. Within four years of graduating from the mentorship program, Ford mobilized his neighbors to establish a large reforestation zone on previously barren, landslide-prone mountainous terrain.

This initiative involved collaborative agreements with landowners, the implementation of soil stabilization techniques such as digging trenches and using vetiver grass for its deep roots and planting eucalyptus trees for compost generation, and the subsequent introduction of fruit trees, hardwoods, and pines. Building on the COPEP Way, Ford facilitated the creation of communal gardens, fostering local food production and enhancing community resilience. The employment generated by the project and the distribution of bonuses distributed three times annually, along with in-kind food bonuses, provide crucial economic support to the participating families. Ford leveraged his earnings to establish a moto-taxi business, further contributing to the local economy while still training his neighbors in sustainable farming. Ford's initiative illustrates how a sense of worth can spur local agency and positive change.

Healthy Birthing

The establishment of a women's health center in 2006 was a response to the reality that cervical cancer is the number one killer of women in Haiti. The center has since expanded its services to address the fact that one out of three women in Haiti were dying in childbirth. As a result, more than 500 babies have now been safely delivered. Comprehensive prenatal and postnatal care are provided for a nominal fee. As Anello emphasizes, "We're now giving women a safe place to deliver a baby, and we're providing good care at low cost to them."

The center's rural location, with the nearest hospitals a considerable distance away, highlights its critical role. Anello points out that in years prior "women were birthing babies at home with either their grandmother or a 'skilled' birthing attendant," often someone with minimal training. The presence of skilled nurses, nurse practitioners from the local nursing school, and an OBGYN has transformed the landscape of women's healthcare in the region. Recognizing broader health challenges in the community, the center has initiated a program to combat hypertension, the second leading cause of death. This screening program is available to both men and women, and crucially, the medicines are free.

Cultivating Hope Through Worth

We derive the following five lessons from what we heard from Anello:

1. Anchor projects in the worthwhileness of real needs: In Haiti, the needs being addressed are as fundamental as life itself.

2. Empower local ownership: When farmers are allowed to own trees they tend, their self-interest matches community's best interest. When healthcare is accessible, people will practice selfcare.

3. Teach useful skills: Create action on a foundation of meaningful education. Learn why planting seeds on hillsides

in the heat is necessary. Learn why pe-natal and post-natal care are lifesaving.

4. Stand together in dignity and purpose: Build community on the collective understanding that every living being matters.

5. Lead with kindness and grit: Anello says, "I tell people to be kind. I tell people to be honest, and I tell people to hold somebody's hand during difficult times."

Anello's reflections on hope are deeply personal. "Hope is forward motion," he says. For him, hope means creating opportunities for others, fostering resilience and showing that even small steps can lead to transformative change. He draws inspiration from his upbringing in a socially conscious family. "My mother was a social worker who always brought people into our home to help them," he recalls. Anello acknowledges the physical and emotional toll of his work but remains steadfast. "Every day in Haiti, my goal is to put a smile on someone's face," he says. "Whether it's telling a joke, giving food, or sharing hope, that's what life is about."

Hope Corrupted

If hope is the desire and search for a future good, attainable though difficult, then what do we call the desire and search for a future evil—or a benefit attained at the expense of others? Can there be hope when worth is absent—or negative?

We might name this "corruption": the desire and search for a future benefit that is self-serving, unjust, or harmful to others, and that is often attained at the cost of the common good. It is the counterfeit of hope, sharing its structure (possible futures, openness to outcomes, collective actions, connections to others) but stripped of worth, stripped of moral content. Corrupted hope mimics hope's energy but not its ethics.

- Hope builds community—corrupted hope segregates and excludes.

- Hope requires belief in shared dignity—corrupted hope thrives on winning in a zero-sum game.

- Hope seeks what is lastingly good—corrupted hope seeks narrow self-interest or worse, victory with vengeance.

But why is it that for every Andy Dufresne, a character in the movie "Shawshank Redemption," who says, "Hope is a good thing, maybe the best of things, and no good thing ever dies," there seems to be an Ellis "Red" Redding who says, in the same movie, "Let me tell you something, my friend. Hope is a dangerous thing. Hope can drive a man insane." For every Shakespeare who praises hope: "Hope is a lover's staff; walk hence with that/And manage it against despairing thoughts," ("The Two Gentlemen of Verona"), there is a Friedrich Nietzsche arguing the other side: "Hope: in reality it is the worst of all evils, because it prolongs the torments of man."

According to Greek mythology, Pandora was the first human woman, created as part of Zeus's punishment for humanity after Prometheus stole fire and gave it to humans. Zeus gave Pandora a box and instructed her never to open it, but she did, releasing all forms of evil and suffering out into the world. Hope, also in the box, remained inside. Some say hope is a divine gift intentionally left behind to help humanity endure the evils that escaped. Others interpret otherwise, saying hope is just another evil, one whose purpose is to prevent humans from accepting reality. The story's enduring power comes from this complexity—hope remains a paradoxical force.

Hope: Blessing Or Curse?

Leaders face a fundamental challenge because, as the psychologist Roy Baumeister and the science journalist John Tierney have documented, "bad is stronger than good." Events, feedback, and experiences that are negative exert a disproportionate influence on how we think and behave, a psychological tendency with deep evolutionary roots that continues to shape organizational life.

Meanwhile, positive psychology has established that focusing exclusively on threats and problems is counterproductive. Better to overbalance bad with good than dwell on the negative. The Losada "critical positivity" ratio introduced by psychologist Barbara Frederickson and mathematician Marcial Losada suggests that flourishing teams maintain approximately three positive interactions for every negative one, indicating that positivity plays a crucial role in high performance.

Whether or not Losada's math checks out, we can vouch for the validity of the underlying principle in any group we have observed. Hopeful groups are many measures more positive than groups mired in dysfunctional aimlessness or fear. At the same time, hopeful groups do not discount fear or look the other way from difficulty or trouble—they have the capacity to "take it all in."

Hope rises above binary perspectives. Hope is a third way, a bridge between seemingly contradictory forces. And unlike blind optimism or resigned fatalism, hope represents a pragmatic middle path—one centered on the concept of worth. Worth manifests in two critical dimensions:

1. Collective Worth: The shared belief that an organization's mission and efforts are meaningful and valuable

2. Individual Worth: Each team member's personal conviction that their contributions matter

When leaders cultivate this dual sense of worth, they enable teams to metabolize negative experiences productively. Hopeful teams are profoundly realistic. And rather than being paralyzed by setbacks or criticism, teams with strong "Hope circuits," as Seligman describes them, can extract learn from difficulties while maintaining forward momentum.

This balanced, bridging approach doesn't deny negativity's power but harnesses it constructively. As Tierney and Baumeister note, we can "rule" the negativity effect rather than being ruled by it. Hope allows organizations to remain clear-eyed about challenges while maintaining positive-to-negative ratios necessary for high performance.

In daily practice, this means creating environments where:

- Negative feedback is delivered constructively within a context of overall support,

- Setbacks are framed as opportunities for learning rather than evidence of failure, and

- The worthiness of both individual contributions and collective goals is paramount.

This we believe wholeheartedly and act on accordingly—Evil, narcissistic or amoral leaders are incapable of true hope. They may speak of the future, but it is a future of conquest, not creation. They may demand loyalty, but they cannot cultivate trust. They can spark movement but not meaning. By positioning hope—grounded in worth—as the mediating force between negativity's pull and positivity's power, leaders can build organizations that are both realistic and resilient, capable of navigating change without succumbing to toxic positivity or debilitating pessimism.

Hope: bridge to better!

In 2003, C. R. Snyder surveyed American businesses and found that the highest hope organizations outperformed others in terms of ROI and growth while exhibiting the following characteristics—a worthy list for any organization to study now and in the future:

- No one, including management, is greatly feared by employees.

- There is a level playing field where everyone has an equal chance to succeed.

- Advancement and benefits are linked to effort expended.

- The "lowest" person in the organization is treated with respect.

- Management's priority is to help employees do the best job possible.

- There is open two-way communication between employees and management.

- Employee feedback is solicited and listened to.

- Decisions are given to employees who are doing the actual work.

- Employees are included in making company goals.

- Employees are given responsibility for finding solutions to problems.

- Employees are the ones who carry out solutions.

- Enduring relationships with customers (long-term goals) are encouraged rather than given sales objectives (short-term goals).

Revisiting these results in 2005, Snyder and his colleagues, Kenneth Rand and Hal Shorey concluded that high-hope companies value inclusive and socially oriented business policies as they "build hope in their host communities and in society at large."

Our take-home message, therefore, is that the tenets of hope theory can be applied not only to produce and sustain healthy financial profits, but also to advance ethical, people-centered conduct in service of the social good.

People want what is worthwhile to them. Meaning and purpose in a work environment where constructive hopes find room to breathe and become real. In a word, people want hope.

Making a Difference

Three years before he became Czechoslovakia's first democratically elected president, Vaclav Havel, a playwright, poet, and political dissident, was asked whether he saw "a grain of hope anywhere in the 1980s." He famously said:

> Hope, in this deep and powerful sense, is not the same as joy that things are going well, or willingness to invest in enterprises that are obviously heading for early success, but, rather, an ability to work for something because it is good, not just because it stands a chance to succeed.

The principle of worth establishes that worthy purposes provide meaning and motivation. When an organization sets goals for itself that are not in its own best interests, people know. Hope's objects must be worthwhile to inspire energy and purpose. The principle of worth at work extends beyond those making an obvious contribution to society: nurses, social workers, teachers, and so on. People find meaning and a sense of calling no matter what their work.

Worth is the substance to hope—you cannot change the world by changing how you think about it. You need to act on its behalf. Congressman John Lewis, the late civil rights leader, is remembered for quoting the African proverb, "When you pray, move your feet." Can you envision a workplace where everyone wants to show up, every day? Where everyone willingly goes the extra mile? Where admirable results are being achieved admirably? To repeat, hope is inherently relational and moral, both motivational and directional.

Here is what Susan Mims, a pediatrician and CEO of Dogwood Health Trust, a charitable foundation serving Western North Carolina, a struggling, mountainous region that has been hammered by floods, winds and fires, told us about how she upholds worth in her job. Dogwood's purpose is this: "We aspire to listen with curiosity to the people in Western North Carolina to inform our stewardship of the resources entrusted to us."

> For me, whether I'm meeting people in the 18 counties and Qualla Boundary we serve, supporting ongoing recovery efforts from Hurricane Helene, working alongside grantees, partners and experts who care about the health and wellbeing of our region, championing equity, mentoring others or serving my state and professional associations, my guiding principle remains my belief in people. When we create fair systems that offer access and opportunity for all, no one has to be left behind.
>
> This sense of value—in the integrity of our work, the dignity of individuals, and the betterment of our world—transcends my personal circumstances or political complexities, driving my commitment to each of these vital roles. Ultimately, it is the pursuit of inherent worth that fuels my dedication, unleashes my dedication to do "whatever it takes" and shapes my purpose for living.

"I want to make a difference," we were told by a leader who may as well have been speaking for everyone we interviewed. Then there was this: "Hope is profound … worth is a precondition." We hope with others and for something good which makes life worth living.

SIX
Embrace Openness

"Hoping does not mean to have a number of hopes at one's disposal. It means, rather, hoping to be open."

Jurgen Moltmann, author of *Theology of Hope*

Openness is the foundation for hope and leadership. Hope is never dialed in to a specific scenario nor is it doctrinaire about a single acceptable outcome. The traditional American spiritual, "Twelve Gates to the City," with its uplifting message that there are multiple points of entry into a solution (or paths to the promised land) and all "tribes" are welcome, is a metaphor for embracing the kind of expansive and inclusive openness that we mean.

Does openness precede upward movement? Openness means not being shut, confined, or sealed. It implies vulnerability, receptivity, accessibility, and freedom from prejudices. In a work environment, openness commissions innovative ideas and authorizes challenges to bias—including confirmation bias, where people close their eyes and ears (and hearts and minds) to "prove" they are right. Hope cares little about all that and instead celebrates discoveries that come from uncertainty—or being wrong.

Openness requires curiosity, the bedrock of learning, and humility, the lifeline of not knowing. Leaders who learn well can lead well. We interviewed curious and humble leaders who could not have been clearer about the value of openness. Openness translates as truth and transparency, welcomed though unexpected outcomes and the joy that comes from innovation and discovery.

- You cannot inspire hope if you are viewed as someone who is not being truthful.

- We are most hopeful at work when the environment is transparent and open.

- When truth abounds, we are more willing to expose more and say more.

- Transparency is the key to hope.

In this chapter we present the story of a courageous team's risky venture into new ways of thinking and the profile of a leader whose legacy is an invitation to be open. Both sketches illustrate the power of hope at work and how openness serves as an essential underlying principle. The context for these examples is not a startup or small creative agency, but a large and successful multinational corporation, yet we believe there is broad application.

The Multicultural Learning Expedition

The story of how Procter and Gamble (P&G) expanded their mainstream brands such as Cover Girl and Max Factor to include the needs of all women, has become lore. Competing companies were beginning to grasp the fact that global majorities were underserved in the US marketplace. P&G had been slow to enlarge its beauty care range.

- Demographics and needs were changing as more women of color entered the market.

- P&G had historically been known for "all-American" cosmetic brands such as Cover Girl.

- A "body parts" way of structuring needed to give way to a holistic, consumer-centric way of understanding people. For example, think of "beauty" instead of "lips."

A small team of savvy professionals within the beauty business, from consumer research to brand and marketing, product development and launch, set out to make a difference. They realized how uniquely sensitive the beauty category is to differences in skin tones and product preferences. When trained in the arts and science of ethnography and organizational learning, they designed a process whose goal was to go beyond the company's superficial culture-specific models in advertising and develop a line of products dedicated to a wider group of consumers.

To understand a broader universe of women's attitudes toward beauty and their beauty care needs, the team grounded themselves in diverse cultures. Their methods were transparently anthropological; they immersed themselves in diverse worlds and worked with people in their homes, neighborhoods, and stores to gain insight that would drive tangible action. They employed contextual methodologies to unleash their curiosity and gain empathy and insight. In their presentations to their colleagues, they quoted former P&G CEO, John Pepper:

> Let us never forget that we are in the business to improve the lives of our consumers. This means we must think like consumers and put ourselves in their shoes. Doing this means that we go beyond understanding consumers. We must understand them and have respect for them as individuals.

In designing the project, one of the team's signal epiphanies was that to be open to what was "out there," they had to begin by being open to what was "in here." That meant confronting their stereotypes and cultural biases, and it required them to become a team that represented multiple aspects of the business and mirrored the three ethnic groups they were studying. The team included a Chinese American product developer, a Black marketer, and a Mexican American ad agency representative. Partnered with White teammates, they brought the voice of their experience into the room and served as cultural guides for the fieldwork.

Getting started, the team, working with Barbara, took a hard look at their personal and cultural biases and beliefs. They established a high degree of comfort and openness with one another and talked about ethnicity in a work setting. Their goal was to begin the fieldwork with open eyes and minds, what psychologist Ellen Langer calls "a mindful state," where thinking is open to creating new categories.

Teams of two visited homes twice. The Black team member and her partner were in Atlanta, the Chinese American and her partner in San

Francisco, and the Mexican American and his partner in Los Angeles. The whole team immersed itself in the cultural milieu of the three cities. In Atlanta, they visited the Martin Luther King historic site and were moved by what they learned about the Civil Rights struggle. When they went to an upscale restaurant, they were underdressed and there were no other White people dining there. In San Francisco, they visited the Chinese Cultural Center, which examines the struggles of early immigrants, and they walked the back streets of Chinatown. There they stumbled into a cookie factory staffed by grandmotherly types who specialized in X-rated fortunes. In Los Angeles they toured Latino neighborhoods. At a swap meet they attracted the unwelcome scrutiny of security guards. They knew they were walking in other people's shoes.

The team learned much about their brands that was relevant to marketing and product development and much that was enlightening. Here is how one person described the experience:

> We all felt that we were changed by this experience. We all came back feeling we had learned something, but more importantly, became a part of something or perhaps something became a part of us? We have enormous energy to represent these groups to our business partners.

Inspired, the team chose to do something we know to be unusual in a corporate context. When they made their final presentation to the company, they related their personal journey. It was a story of openness, courage, and hope. Knowing they now shared an experience and voice within the organization for a newly recognized group of customers, they felt an enhanced sense of responsibility and agency—and trepidation.

Here are the words of a participant, with hope's principle of connection being realized at the launch. They could not have forecast that systemic connections would ensue, organizational processes and structures would evolve, departments and functions would break out of silos, and unexpected alliances with vendors and competitors would occur.

> When "The Ethnic Learning Expedition" was formed, the team that came together was enthusiastic about the project because it was the RIGHT thing to do, I was excited to be part of the team and ready to discover more about these people. I had never done anything like this before: going right into people's homes and their lives.

Doing the "right thing," having a direct line of sight to peoples' lives and knowing you can make a difference—hope's principle of worth—enabled courage.

> I really didn't know much about these people. I was uncomfortable because I didn't know very much and was a little anxious about how I would be received in their homes. Would I intrude on their lives? Would I be respectful or accidentally disrespectful? How would I be treated? Would they isolate me or even speak to me on a personal level because I'm different than they are?

The principle of openness came into play as perceptions and biases were explored without defensiveness or shame. That was their work. Not pie-in-the-sky wishful thinking or intuition, but grounded insights that are technologically feasible.

> To prepare for this adventure, I explored my own perceptions and biases about this group and identified them. I wanted to

make myself aware by opening my mind and heart. I wanted to see and hear what they experience. I wanted to walk in their shoes and peek into their lives.

Having the wherewithal to make a difference in bringing about a better future through personal voice, functional voice, and the voice of the customer, engaged the principle of agency.

So off I went with my tape recorder and camera to explore their homes, their neighborhoods, and their lives. I immersed myself in their worlds, and then, something unexpected started to happen. Suddenly, as I stood there in the homes, on the streets, and in the worlds of these people, I became them. I felt what it was like to be them.

Hope at work: the universal truth that people are people, united in the human condition:

I realized how disconnected I was from the way they live their lives. How little I or anyone really knew about these people. BUT YOU KNOW WHAT? They weren't so unlike me after all. We connected on a human level that made all these differences seem trivial. I felt a kinship with them that changed my perceptions I had so carefully listed when I started my journey.

The team's presentation to leadership had four sections. The first three were descriptions of the beauty values, rituals and lifestyles of the three groups they immersed themselves in. Their fourth section was most unusual in the P&G context. It was named, "Do We Have the Courage to Make a Difference?"

The team had taken a risk. They had doubts and fears. They knew they were bringing new voices promoting makeup for diverse skin palettes. They talked about their personal Odysseys and transformations in doing the study. Along the way, this way of seeing became who they were, and they continued doing the same thing with other projects for years afterward.

"I didn't think of it as hope," we were told when Barbara talked with participants afterward. Hope was not a lens applied at the time. No matter. We think the outward and visible signs showed hope at work.

Opening Inward, Opening Out

The P&G story of contextual research in beauty care teaches how hope can accrue on several levels at once. There is a desire on the part of the company and its managers to enter a new market profitably. Good new products will satisfy new customers, creativity will be rewarded in pursuit of those new products, and cross-cultural sensitivity will be acknowledged for its role in directing innovation. Careers will be assisted and perhaps lives will be changed. This is what the speaker quoted above concluded:

> I felt a sense of shame because our job is to improve the lives of the world's consumers, yet not everything we do is in the best interests of these people that I came to know. I want to make a difference but I'm afraid. Am I now the minority in a culture that doesn't have the same understanding that I now do? Am I alone in my desire to improve their lives? Do we have the courage to make a difference?

Even today, we are moved by the poignancy and profundity of this revelation spoken by a marketing researcher two decades ago. Being open to what was "in here" as well as what was "out there" worked a certain magic. The unexpected happened, and the process unfolded in a way that was neither conscious nor linear, benefitting all who were touched by it.

According to Lisa Reynolds, who was Brand Manager of Multicultural Cosmetics, the ethnography work led into a huge breakthrough—cosmetics for women of color. In partnership with Queen Latifah, P&G launched Cover Girl's Queen line, a pioneering line of makeup specifically for darker skin tones. This was a major step towards inclusivity in the beauty industry and paved the way for many other brands to offer a wider range of shades.

We believe the greatest barrier to openness, as described above, is fear. In our interviews, we were told repeatedly how being afraid blocks action and truth-telling. We have felt and witnessed moments when saying "I don't know" might have been a career-limiting statement.

Fear is present in mundane ways—when people are afraid to let others see what they don't know, or fearful of being misunderstood and held lacking, or unwilling to reveal what they really think, or scared of the consequences of speaking truth to power. Without safety on the outside there can be no safety on the inside.

The easily understood (though not easily applied) concept of psychological safety is central to this discussion. In 1965, leadership and organizational culture elders Edgar Schein and Warren Bennis wrote "Psychological safety reduces a person's anxiety about being basically accepted and worthwhile, allowing for more open participation in learning and change." Lack thereof yields all manner of anti-social behavior and organizational cost. Here a leader describes how relative freedom can be safe:

> We take risks and look for new paths to get this organization more open to the changing marketplace and changing business model. It doesn't come naturally to get out of our comfort zone. It can be very threatening to others, but to me it's exciting. I will push then see when to back off. People go through different stages before becoming more comfortable. It's going a little slower than I'd like but we'll get there.

Hope holds the thread from openness to engagement, from discovery to delivery—of deodorant and dental floss!

Consumer is Boss

Soon after A.G. Lafley became CEO of P&G, his watchword, "consumer is boss," codified in the formula, "C=B," became a lasting legacy. The importance of C=B is that it flipped the organizational pyramid upside down, with consumers at the top, consumer-facing P&G-ers next, and the CEO at the bottom. And it is easily remembered.

Lafley invited marketing and product development functions, all business units and a growing list of partners to take risks and venture beyond their perceived boundaries in location or categories of thinking. He demanded they deliver consumer-driven insights and results. Lafley's passion for innovation has been internalized at P&G.

> I think you must be inherently hopeful and trusting, and I think it takes courage. I always believed that somehow, some way, if we interacted with our consumers in the right way, with enough of the right people and the right resources, we would understand them better than they really understood themselves.

Lafley lived the belief that a company should never outsource its eyes and ears. He was a role model for direct, immersive learning in the customer's context. He put himself and his leaders "out there" on a regular basis. He articulated the goal and set the example. He was a beacon of openness.

> In the past we often approached customers with very narrow objectives in mind: to learn how they washed their hair or cleaned their clothes. We should still look for these insights, but from a much broader vantage point. It's important to get into the consumers' lives, to know what their entire day or week or month is like, to understand how they juggle all the priorities of their lives, to get a glimpse of how they enjoy the solitude of quiet moments at the end of their day. This is the best way to discover how we can make a particular moment in their daily lives a little better, easier, more enjoyable.

Those words when spoken 25 years ago were radical indeed. Though ethnography is now in everyone's toolkit in some form, Lafley's level of commitment stands out. Recently he told us, "Our job is to touch lives and improve lives in brief daily experiences with our brands and products. I used to say, 'We're not curing cancer, but we are making daily household and personal care moments a little better.'"

Lafley knows too that even when consumers are meticulously listened to, they have difficulty describing what they want or need. A prototype (a rough package or product) or a concept (an idea or a picture) can stimulate an actionable response. Then it can become a product in a package with a price. Nevertheless. The process begins with cultural and corporate commitment to openness.

Once we understood that what we're doing is touching you for a few moments a day—whether it's the seconds it takes for you to put on a deodorant or the minutes to brush and floss your teeth—it was our hope that our connection with the consumer would be a win for the consumer and would work out for us over time.

The Hope Meister

Lafley had to lead through crises while at P&G, multiple times: 9/11 and natural disasters. "If you were in the middle of it, it could create a lot of fear." In each case it was "first things first": Get employees, their families and their communities back on their feet, feeling safe and secure and provided with food and shelter. And "only then did we return to work, which they wanted to do. It meant returning to a more hopeful world than what had preceded."

In 2000, Lafley experienced one of the most challenging moments in his 36 years at P&G. After his first quarter as CEO, they completely missed the earnings estimate and the stock price dropped in half, in half a day. Everyone, from the people in the cafeteria to the executives in the corporate headquarters, was part of the profit-sharing trust program, and their profit-sharing trust accounts were cut in half overnight.

> I remember standing on a chair in the hallway in the middle of the open offices on the beauty and personal care floor of the general office building. I was leading the North American businesses, and I just started up beauty care business. And I stood on this chair because people were running around watching the stock price go down on TV monitors installed throughout the building.

Simple truths became touchstones of hope amid uncertainty.

> I said, you know what? We sold as much or more Tide today. Consumers did as many loads of laundry today. We sold as many diapers today as we did yesterday. We sold as much Crest toothpaste, and as much Pantene and Olay. I just went through the brands, and I said you understand that the stock market is an expectations game... but when I finished it dropped another $6!

> And later, in June, when I had become CEO, the stock dropped again. By the time I was in the chair for 30 days, the stock price had gone from $118 to $52. I'm not going to tell you that people weren't afraid.

> My job for my first 100 days was Reality Seeker/Understander, and Hope Meister.

Repeating simple truths with all stakeholders broadcast openness and restored hope.

> I was constantly on the go meeting employees and customers. Suppliers wanted to know if they were going to get paid. I went out and started seeing the big grocers and they said, what are you doing here? Isn't your company falling apart? Shouldn't you be at headquarters? And I said don't worry. Whatever you need, we're going to have it on your shelf tomorrow.

> I wanted to be out with consumers, shoppers, customers, grocers, and suppliers to ensure everyone that P&G would deliver what they needed.

"Peddling hope" does not require having all the facts at hand, not does it rest on being completely self-assured.

> I was sort of 70 percent confident, but I didn't have insight into financial, operational or executional realities when they put me in the job. I buried myself for a couple of weekends with the treasurer, the accountants, the controller. Hey, take me through the balance sheet, the income statement, the sales and profit forecast, line-by-line. Tell me how much money we have in these banks? How much cash, you know all that kind of stuff.

> But in the beginning, I was peddling hope.

Lafley's approach illustrates a vital leadership lesson. During crises, leaders must embody and communicate hope—it comes with the job. "I don't say things I don't believe," he stresses. Instead, he draws on real, tangible stories to comfort and encourage, crafting a narrative that could motivate others to see beyond immediate setbacks.

> I talked about things I was sure of: We did sell as much or more Tide. I always looked for things that were reassuring and factual, which bolstered my hope. These anecdotes became stories to tell our people, our team, our employees, and our partners, customers and suppliers. I became the prophet of hope.

Lafley affirms the power of hope—not as a naive ideal, but as a deliberate, actionable force where openness is an underlying principle.

For Lafley, and at P&G, hope runs deep. He drew wisdom and strength from what he knew of Richard Deupree (1885-1974), a man who had worked his way up from the mailroom to become the first non-family member appointed president and board chair. Deupree led P&G through the Great Depression and World War II. He is known to have said that if you take away all company's products, manufacturing plants and buildings, but you leave our people, we will build everything back again within ten years.

> What he was saying rang true for me. I put faith in the customer. And I deeply believed in our people. Those were the sources of my hope. When we put the right people against the right problem or the right opportunity, somehow, someway, they figure it out. I had tremendous hope and faith in our people and, and I think that was honestly that's about all I had.

Through crises, innovation, and cultural shifts, leadership rooted in hope can drive lasting success. Hope Meisters offer timeless lessons for anyone seeking to lead with purpose and possibility.

The un-CEO

In 2002, after just two years as head of P&G, having orchestrated a revitalization in a company that seemingly had lost its way, *FORTUNE* magazine spent a week observing Lafley on his rounds attending strategy meetings, inspecting manufacturing plants and visiting stores. *FORTUNE* concluded that he fit a "new breed" of turnaround leader: the "un-CEO." Lafley, it seemed, unlike many others who achieved lofty ranks and roles elsewhere, did not speak about having a "grand vision." He talked softly and asked questions. "He's a listener, not a storyteller.

He's likable but not awe inspiring. He's the type of guy who gets excited in the mop aisle of a grocery store."

In an age when corporate leaders often gravitated towards assertive commands, Lafley, embodied a refreshing contrast, and he still does. He is a leader who views himself foremost as an employee, someone who thrives on principles of integrity, mutual trust, and shared hope.

At P&G, Lafley found himself aligned with a company steeped in values. Integrity— "do the right thing"—and mutual trust formed the bedrock of its culture. He believes these principles are inherently hopeful: "If you trust your colleagues and partners to do the right thing, positive outcomes follow."

Lafley's admiration for P&G extended to its historical commitment to employees. He notes the company's early adoption of an all-employee profit-sharing plan in the 1920s, sustained even during the Great Depression. This gesture of ownership and shared success exemplified a hopeful and trusting worldview. This is what he told us—and we believe he has been saying similar things for decades: "Learning based on consumer and customer engagement and involvement and then spirited dialogue to translate what we're learning into better decisions, definitely improves organizational performance and results in more sustainable success."

After two rounds as CEO at P&G and successful leadership tours in nonprofit, academic, and startup realms, Lafley retains his humility, steadfast values and disarmingly approachable style. Having known him since college days, Harry can say he is consistent to his core. What is the inside-out fuel that relentlessly feeds his fire for outside-in? Now in his 70s, he is staying "open."

Lafley's journey began in a small, semi-rural community. The Lafley name is la fleur, the flower (a French name for soldiers or servants). They came from Montreal, Quebec. Two brothers married Mohawk Indian sisters in Montreal and walked across the border into Enosburg

Falls, VT, in the 1860s. Later there were marriages into Irish families in Boston.

Growing up in a family of third-generation immigrants, optimism was a defining trait. "My grandparents came to the United States because it was a beacon of hope," he reflects. Their gratitude for this new land shaped a family culture centered on positivity and perseverance. This ethos was reinforced during his school years, where competing against larger schools taught him resilience. "We didn't go into games expecting to lose," he recalls.

The attitude that better outcomes are possible became a cornerstone of his leadership philosophy. Lafley often emphasizes the importance of choosing a hopeful path over a fearful one, a principle he credits with guiding his decision-making in life and business. Lafley's orientation to make choices and make the best of those choices—or make new choices!—is a mainstay of hope.

> There are moments throughout your life from the beginning of life when you have opportunities to choose the hopeful path or the fearful path. The positive path or the negative path, the optimistic path, the pessimistic path. And so, you ask yourself, well when were those moments and what choices did I make ... and why?

His father, Alan F. Lafley, flew in the Pacific as a navigator, and thanks to the GI Bill, went to college and business school and into a Ph.D. program. He worked at General Electric for twenty years followed by several at Clark Equipment and ten at Chase Manhattan Bank. In 2009, (A.G.) Lafley sent Harry a bound volume of his father's interviews and presentations while in human resources, inscribed: "My father's early take on HR concepts, principles, and practices still relevant and important today. Hopefully, of interest."

Several themes from the father's HR career have played out in the son's tenure as a CEO—identification of talent at all levels, leader-led management development, professional growth of underrepresented employees, on-the-job-learning, teamwork, and collaboration. When Lafley was in business school, he wrote a case on "The Role of HR" which described his father's approach. He concluded that, "The success factors are ... simple and straightforward"—personal credibility, pragmatism, and taking initiative, "not to gain power and control for their own sakes," but to solve problems and get things done.

Lafley draws lessons from his ancestors and origins, and he is grateful and positive about who he is. Indeed, his humble self-confidence must derive in part from recollection of his family legacy and lifelong self-reflection. As such, Lafley has been courageous in facing unfriendly realities and being open to new information and paradigms. Witness his inclination to "turn the pyramid upside down" with the consumer at the top and him at the bottom. His pragmatic, people-first orientation underlies how he characterizes himself as a Hope Meister. On the authority of our interviews and research, we conclude that Lafley is at once a catalyst for optimism, a resilient leader, a connector and listener, and an encourager of growth.

There really is no "secret sauce" at P&G. The "P&G way" is there for all to see. Open conversations produced a better understanding of the marketplace, better decisions, and more ownership of those decisions. The pressure to achieve consumer-driven insights is always there in the company. What better way to achieve results than to become an organizational learning machine?

Openness Day by Day

To be clear, our findings do not suggest that radical openness is always the best answer—nor is directness or speed of decision-making or even telling the truth. To suggest a formula for being open would denigrate the complexities of leadership and trivialize hope. Context is crucial. Misreading a moment can be disastrous. Well-intentioned gullibility is never a virtue.

Hope requires leaders to be canny and shrewd, as in these quotations:

- I'm respectful of others and their ideas. Assuming positive intent, making the charitable assumption, you're really open to possibility. But it's a fine balance of being open to outcomes and needing to make a decision.

- This is tricky. When you're an executive and see bad times ahead, you have to be careful how you communicate and still keep hope alive. How much do you communicate? When and how? We tell the truth, but maybe not until asked, and then we tell the truth with optimism based on our experience and beliefs.

- I'm an open book, and I have an open-door policy. I always give benefit of the doubt first. Sometimes it's painful to be open. I'm not naïve, but I do get burned.

Hope Meisters are unsentimental and resolute, strategic and wise. They make decisions to advance a vision while staying adaptable. There is always a danger in overthinking a situation, taking in too many factors and getting stuck. To conclude this chapter, we return to fundamentals and quote others we interviewed:

- Be open to admitting what you don't know and to new approaches.

- Welcome collective discovery.

- Show your feelings and thinking as a leader.

- Be willing to visualize the future outside existing paradigms.

- I watch body language. I have certain people who are my bellwethers. I know who has a lot of capacity, and I feel and watch their stress. Sometimes I have no choice, but often I do. I can back off, or I can jump in and surround them with support.

Openness enables collaboration, creativity, and change. We say, openness generates "spiritual elbowroom" while honoring allegiances to knowledge and truth.

Where you work is more likely than not to be different from Procter & Gamble, and you may not completely relate to A.G. Lafley's brand of leadership. We say that whoever you are, wherever you are, and whenever you choose, there is enormous value in openness—listening to what people have to say, perhaps turning hierarchy on its head, welcoming new ideas—which allows core values, timeless principles, and proven leadership practices to thrive.

Consider how much it matters, at work, to feel bracingly alive, curious and yet confident about whatever might happen next. We know it matters, a lot. This is openness, the foundation for hope.

Openness in the Balance

We conclude with a note of moderation—lest we lose readers who may be thinking, "Yes, but ... ." "Too much" openness on almost any front at work is unnatural and can be daunting if not terrifying. Discomfort related to lack of structure and fear of the unknown, can cause workers to experience work aversion, known as "ergophobia." In our experience, open dialogue, unstructured activities, or prolonged silence may be a source of anxiety for most anyone.

Of course, too little openness, at the other extreme, is the organizational enemy we target in this chapter. Perhaps having "minimum critical specifications" for projects at work, where essential outcomes are agreed while "how-tos" are not, is a good way to encourage "safe openness." You may well have other techniques in mind.

Getting the balance right when it comes to openness is an essential task for leaders. Perfectionism and uncompromising rigidity are not anyone's prescriptions for effective leadership behavior; neither is laisse-faire behavior, inattention, or looking the other way.

Hope is both principled and paradoxical. Embracing openness requires trust and risk. Hope thrives in ambiguity.

SEVEN
Establish Connection

"Only Connect ... Live in fragments no longer."

E.M. Forster, writer and public intellectual renowned for his searching explorations of human connection

Connection harmonizes hope. When people are grounded in who they are and in alignment on where they want to go, and when they are aligned on why they work together, they can advance towards a preferred future. Establishing connection coordinates the other four principles—openness, possibility, worth and agency—to achieve sustained progress.

In a summary of nearly 100 years of happiness research the social science researcher Sonja Lyubomirsky said, "I would say that 95 percent of things that are effective in making people happy ... are because they make people feel more connected to other people." In this chapter, we argue that establishing connection does more than achieve happiness; it enables complex, hopeful work.

Connection in Northeastern University

Richard O'Bryant is the Chief Belonging Officer at Northeastern University, promoted into a role he helped design in 2024 because he sensed an opportunity and a need.

The opportunity he saw is to extend the university's identity as a unique cooperative educational alternative to traditional learning and build a sense of loyalty to the entire institution. O'Bryant aspires to increase connection within the large and diverse culture at Northeastern: thirteen campuses and partner institutions, 38,000 students with connections to 70 countries, 1,500 faculty, 15,000 staff, and coop programs in 50 countries.

The need at Northeastern is to bring clarity to the confusing crosscurrents of identities, protests, and uncertainties happening at all levels and interests of the institution—students, staff, faculty, administration, and alumni. O'Bryant, in his rapidly expanding role, is being pulled into issues that come up against barriers or that cross boundaries in multiple directions. One day he may be interpreting the impacts of policy changes or advising on staffing issues; on another day he is coordinating programs with the Oakland, California campus; or he is counseling students worried about their Pell Grants; or he is being a sounding board to advocacy groups; or he is lending support to mentoring programs for junior faculty. His is the voice of reason and compassion, and he is sought by many.

O'Bryant has reimagined his function to be broad-based, inclusive, interactive, and comprehensive—from "we'll teach you" (expert model) to "we'll build it together" (engagement model). His role is not DEI under a new name. His greatest value is not teaching or training or enforcing compliance. It is listening, mediating, and searching for common ground.

Richard O'Bryant is following an example set by his late father. John D. O'Bryant, a significant civil rights leader, politician and educator in Boston, whose "prolific" contributions influenced President Carter, Governor Michael Dukakis, and Senator Edward Kennedy. At Northeastern, he became the first African American appointed vice president of the university. In recognition of his contributions to the city, Boston Technical High School was renamed the John D. O'Bryant School of Mathematics and Science. Richard O'Bryant continues to honor his father's legacy in new and profound ways.

As a concrete example of his work, O'Bryant recently conceived, designed, and facilitated a four-hour virtual meeting, "A Vision of Belonging at Northeastern Conference," with 100 participants from all corners of the university. Students, faculty, and staff, convened to stake out a vision for belonging where everyone feels attached and appreciative. Belonging was defined as both a process and aspirational goal and described variously as "the ability to see and be seen," "mattering," and "when a community is invested in you and when you are invested in the community."

One of the hard lessons that emerged, in the words of a student, is that, "It's hard to feel hopeful if you don't feel you belong." While emphasizing the value of "mindful curiosity," meeting participants were challenged to interact with people they do not know and to wonder about ways to "make things better" for people who might feel they do not belong. Establishing connection means "little things matter," such as being observant about others' likes and dislikes, and being devoted to a big picture—in this case the university itself. A striking finding of the conference was that "students just want to be believed" and not be second-guessed or discounted when facing problems and seeking support.

Seven opportunities for action were identified in the conference: regularly engaging students, enhancing affinity group support, developing better mentorship programs, improving cross-campus relationships, elevating staff voices, establishing transparent support processes, and creating more cross-campus engagement. Two insights were:

1. Fostering belonging is everyone's responsibility, and not the responsibility of a single office or initiative, and

2. Faculty and staff must themselves experience belonging to be able to support students.

O'Bryant is on a mission to embrace what he sees as "The Village of Belonging: From A to A"—from Applicants to Alums.

Connecting You to You

Just as Richard O'Bryant is inspired by his father's legacy and his family's values, you must be connected to who you are to build bridges to others. Being who you are requires knowing who you are. "Know Thyself," Harry's college motto, an inscription on the Temple of Delphi, speaks to age-old wisdom.

When we speak together as the team of Barbara and Harry, we speak often about our ancestors, inheritances, and ideas passed on from elders. Barbara prioritizes her annual pilgrimages to Greece above all other travel. Her DNA starts with a tiny pinpoint at the southern-most tip of mainland Greece, the Mani, a rugged, isolated peninsula between mountains and the sea. Raised bilingually, filled with stories from grandparents who emigrated, her roots there go back hundreds of years. Fifty years ago, she lived there for a year wanting to discover, as Zorba the Greek says, "what the blood remembers." She has returned many times since with children and grandchildren.

The sense of belonging she feels in that small village is her life force. She is known by and knows three generations of families. To walk the stone paths her ancestors walked, to touch the small church they built centuries ago, to soak in the light, the sea, the air, the olive oil, and the genuine welcome, tells her she is at home. Always, this trip is a pilgrimage of profound healing—body, mind, and spirit.

Harry is a Life Member of the Genealogical Society of Allegany County, Maryland. Some of his ancestors worked in local coal mines owned by other ancestors. Relatives worked for the Baltimore and Ohio Railroad and at the giant paper mill in Luke, Maryland. In cemeteries ten miles apart, one grandfather, born in 1869, is at rest in Keyser, West Virginia, while a great grandfather, born in the same year, is memorialized up McMullen Highway in the Hutson Cemetery in Rawlings, Maryland. Harry sees these and other clues as influences on his career in employee relations, his hobby driving steam trains, and his love of art that depicts factories and mines. His aim is to understand his own predilections and preferences and to be more welcoming of the ways of others.

"For me, the place of my ancestors is the place of my heart. When I think of home, I think of that place of belonging," wrote the public intellectual and cultural critic, bell hooks. To belong is to be free to be fully oneself, to live in alignment with one's values, and to be part of a community that honors that wholeness.

Our colleague Jerry Colonna emphasizes "radical self-inquiry" as a fundamental pathway to authentic self-understanding. Colonna's recent book, *Reunion: Leadership and the Longing to Belong*, is at once a personal memoir, leadership guide, and manifesto for courage and compassion in service of a more hopeful world—and world of work. Colonna's process involves deep personal examination and awareness as a prerequisite for authentic connection and community building. It begins with you asking, Who am I? (How do I identify?) Then, Whose am I? (What are my origins—the ties that bind?) And third, What is my unique work to do? (How can I contribute to this place we all call home?) The crux is Colonna's insight that "your story is my story." "Reuniting with the reality of your ancestral journeys—however unpleasant they may feel—will open you to the possibility of seeing that the others' story is, in the end, your story." Reunion is a reconnection with oneself—through others.

Relationship Building

We have been working together, and writing about hope, for more than 30 years. We are students of many of the same mentors; we share clients and sources of wisdom; we console each other after significant losses and medical traumas. We were born in the same hospital, on different dates, in Iowa. We enjoy both bourbon and Bourbon Street. We both taught social studies in public high school. We love to laugh at ourselves and make fun of absurdities. It goes on.

And we are very different in very significant ways. Barbara is an urbanite who prefers to live in rural oases among the trees. Harry is a suburbanite who prefers towns with sidewalks. More profoundly, although both of us are practicing "hopesters," Barbara approaches hope more experientially, Harry more conceptually. When Harry gets confused, he becomes sad. When something goes sideways with Barbara, she gets mad. We are headstrong and skeptical, and we do not duck advice posted on the wall at the United Ministries of Durham, NC, a shelter for unhoused people: "Be humble. You may be wrong."

Why does this matter in a book about hope? Because relationship-building—establishing, maintaining, and evolving interpersonal connection with those with whom we choose to live, work, and play—is bedrock. One of the sources of our professional pride is that we consult to clients who have known for decades. Our life purposes include leaving a legacy in our field that we have created together. We do not take hope lightly.

ESTABLISH CONNECTION

Meaningful relationship-building offers hope among friends and families, acquaintances and strangers, and colleagues at work. At Stanford University, "Touchy-Feely," the nickname for a course in interpersonal dynamics, has been the most popular offering in the MBA program for years. In their book, *Connect: Building Exceptional Relationships with Family, Friends, and Colleagues*, David Bradford and Carole Robin, teachers and course-developers, share stories and practical lessons that can benefit anyone who is serious about hope at work. A core concept is that an ability to recognize, regulate, and respond wisely to feelings and emotions—your own and others—makes it possible for you to connect with people in almost any context.

At the end of their book, Bradford and Robin reveal how a twenty-year relationship can go awry—theirs. In heartfelt detail they write about an incident that nearly ended their high-trust colleagueship and friendship, and how they used the principles in their book to recover and repair.

Our precipitating incident was a period of exasperation when writing this book, born of physical separation, competing priorities, and differences in how we handle conflict. For those of you who have truly co-authored something as weighty as a book and one laden with personal meaning and mission, you know how hard that can be. Barbara had delivered to Harry a sheaf of her most recent work and an electronic version, and was down the road, as it were, waiting for a response.

Harry had gone missing. After several weeks, Barbara wrote in an email:

> When you were here, I presented you with a little bundle of what I have been working at for months. Much of which you had never seen before. I did not get one word of acknowledgement, feedback, love it, hate it, NOTHING. Crickets. I don't know if you even read it. Considering you are supposedly my

co-author; I have no idea where your head is at except being perpetually very busy and distracted. I have absolutely no clue where this work falls on your "to do" list or among your many commitments.

He was indeed distracted by life and work and also flummoxed. He had skimmed but not reviewed her recent contribution, because he did not know what he thought or wanted to do or say, and he felt regretful and embarrassed about not producing much writing of his own. He had done little more than some formatting. Worse, Harry criticized Barbara's formatting of his own most recent work.

And one more thing, Barbara deserves credit for initiating the current book project and inspiring Harry to accomplish "meaningful work that allows you to make a difference." Deservedly, and characteristically, Barbara wrote how she felt "frustrated and frankly hurt," and more: "hugely disrespected." She was ANGRY. Harry had felt her being pissed off before, aimed at him or others, and he knew there were always valid grounds for her fury. In fact, Harry admires her ability to express white heat and then realize its upside: clarifying what matters, enhancing self-understanding, fueling motivation for action, and strengthening relationships. For years, Harry has preached that intimacy resides on the other side of conflict. Here was a case in point.

Barbara had his complete attention now, and he wrote back:

> I'm out of town again and in an Uber headed to a meeting. Home tomorrow and I get my life back. You're right on all points. I've dropped out of sight on the book. I'm sorry and I'm sorrier that I've hurt you. I can reengage on Saturday. Then several weeks of prioritizing our book. It's been two months of

too much work and travel. Neglected exercise and done only what was in front of my nose. Not an excuse. And not smart. This will be a joy to read. I'll be back.

To which she said: "🖤 🖤 always and forever."
And he said: "You caused a tear."
And she wrote, "🖤 🖤 🖤 🖤."

Our episode is not meant to illustrate an archetypal blow-up—it was more like a "pinch" threatening to become a "crunch." Nor is it meant to explain how two parties in a relationship are equally culpable when there is a difficulty. Harry owns the weighted responsibility in this set-to, and in retrospect he is grateful that it happened. Barbara was generous in her behavior toward him, and Harry feels closer to her than ever.

Instead, the story is one of resilience in individuals and in relationships and how the wisdom in being touchy-feely can be accessed and applied and perhaps brought to bear even when interactions are seemingly normal and smooth. On reflection, what we did to restore our relationship reflexively might well have come from the book. This is what comes to mind:

- We were both willing to be vulnerable.
- We were honest expressing how we felt.
- We trusted that we could deal productively with our conflict.
- We were forgiving.
- We were kind to each other and ourselves.

No doubt, there will be more friction and more for us to unpack—when you are in pursuit of "exceptional relationships," and writing books together, there always is. For us, the through line of the story and the bottom line of our relationship is our deep and caring connection to each other.

Ensemble/Artificial Intelligence

Increasingly complex challenges at work require new organizational designs that are less reliant on the means of control—efficiency, standardization, and hierarchy—and more oriented toward flexibility, creativity, and ownership. As Artificial Intelligence streamlines the workforce, the workplace, and the work itself, self-directed groups, such as ensembles—as in musical performance—present hopeful models for connection

Harvey Seifter, a classically trained musician and orchestra leader, was executive director of the conductor-less Orpheus Orchestra when they won Grammy Awards. The mission statement of Orpheus, from 1972, incorporates democratic principles in their rehearsals and performances: Musicians take ownership, they rotate leadership roles, and their rehearsals are dialogues—fostering creative satisfaction among players. "When you're playing in Orpheus, your voice matters," reports a violinist. "You're not just playing the notes—you're shaping the music."

In medicine, surgical teams, trauma teams, and labor and delivery teams are examples where high-stakes performance occurs without a single hierarchical leader. Similarly: flight deck operators on aircraft carriers, film production crews, restaurant kitchen brigades, and agile software developers. These collaborative work designs typically share common elements: pressurized tasks, need for rapid adaptation, complexity in coordination, reliance on expertise, dependence on flexibility—and minimal reliance on command-and-control.

According to Seifter, multileader groups such as these, are ensembles, and they are better suited to many situations than traditional teams. He defines an ensemble as "a small group of people who work closely together to accomplish a shared purpose, and who together produce a single outcome that could not possibly be accomplished by one person working alone." Ensemble intelligence creates a system where leadership emerges from expertise and context, supported by strong collaborative practices and organizational culture. The ensemble model creates a more resilient, adaptive, and innovative culture of work, while developing leadership capacity among everyone.

Alvin Toffler predicted in 1970, writing in *Future Shock*, that as technology becomes more pervasive, we will experience a greater need for human connection. Without balancing high-tech with high-touch, he argued, we will be traumatized by future technological innovations. Lest we confuse tasks with jobs, and data with desires, we need human tools to manage AI tools.

Our colleague John Winsor and his compatriots, Jen Stave, who is also at Harvard's Digital Data, and Design Institute, and Ryan Kurt, a generative AI expert at Salesforce, report that AI agents have changed the workforce. They have graduated from being sidekicks for human workers to becoming digital teammates. Organizations must act now, these experts say, to redesign workflows and rearrange business models to attract and retain talent—and to enable humans and AI agents to work well together. Reprising Alvin Toffler, the authors conclude with a hopeful reminder of "human centricity" at work.

While AI can handle many tasks more quickly than humans, your enterprise still relies on the insight, empathy, and relationships that only people can deliver. By maintaining this dual focus—on unleashing AI's efficiency and safeguarding human creativity—you stand the best chance of driving sustainable growth.

D. Graham Burnett, an historian of science and technology, reports on his experiments in classes of undergraduates at Princeton on how to use AI. Rather than forbidding its use, he has encouraged it. Anti-AI policies on campus have "paralyzed" students. He asked a class to engage one of the new AI tools and explore what they could do. "Reading the results, on my living-room couch, turned out to be the most profound experience of my teaching career." The results were "astonishing." In one instance, where a student asked the system to write a song that would make someone cry, Burnett found himself crying. Other student results "stripped his wildest imaginings."

Burnett's sense-making is what concerns us here. AI, as he conceives it, may be a "conceptual win" for the humanities. Machines can manipulate the "total archive" of human knowledge, which frees you up to look inward and ask yourself the important questions about your life and the lives of others. If we are to conclude that AI can accomplish tasks but not jobs, and can provide answers without making meaning, it sets the stage for ensemble intelligence—throwing us back into connection with each other.

The conductor is not the enemy in a musical ensemble, nor is any boss or powerful authority figure a villain in performing collaborative work. Ensemble intelligence does not denigrate leadership. It distributes it differently, favoring knowledge- and skill-based contribution over political direction, and fluid and situational hierarchy over the static and role-based. In an ensemble, anyone can be a leader, which may mean that everyone will be a follower. Skilled leaders bring vision, inspire collaboration, and exercise good judgement. Ensembles embrace hope.

The Truth About Truth

In a disconnected world, the phrase, "alternative facts," is intended to justify dubious positions and demonize opponents. Hope requires a different outlook. The philosophical principle of charity says you should assume that the positions of others are coherent and rational, even when you disagree—not only as an ethical stance, but because it enables communication across differences and divides.

In the 1990s, when A.G. Lafley was working for P&G in Japan, he studied Total Quality Management under W. Edwards Deming. One of Deming's thought leaders told him, "We know when a company has achieved TQM when its employees tell management the truth." Here is Lafley:

> You know, or you think you know (or, to make a point, you think you think you know) when you are being told the truth by management or by each other. There is scientific evidence that when truth resonates, a positive physiological response follows.

"I feel you," as they say in Harry's hometown of Baltimore. Our shorthand is to say that when truth enters the room, hope follows.

The truth about what you perceive as "real truth," however, is subject to significant limitations and cognitive biases. For example, there is the well-known phenomenon called "confirmation bias," where you tend to remember information that confirms your preexisting beliefs, and you downplay evidence to the contrary. There is also the "illusory truth effect," where your repeated exposure to a lie can make it seem more accurate. And when there are gaps in your understanding, you tend to make things up. There are many more of these. Our simple proxy here is to say that your gut is right only about half the time.

The psychologist and professor Jamil Zaki distinguishes skepticism, which encompasses inquiry, doubt, and devil's advocacy, from cynicism, the theory that people are selfish, greedy and dishonest. In *Hope for Cynics: The Surprising Science of Human Goodness*, he writes, "Cynics end up sicker, sadder, poorer, and more wrong." Zakil's concept is that having high faith in people and high faith in data is a formula for being a hopeful skeptic—in a word, being highly connected to truth and the bearers of truth.

Cynics are more likely to promulgate and be taken in by "post-truth"—more likely to accept arguments based on their emotions and beliefs rather than those grounded in factual evidence. Hopeful skeptics, on the other hand, speak to heart and head. "More than ever," writes Mathew d'Ancona, former editor of the *Spectator*, in one of many current books about post-truth, "Truth requires an emotional delivery system that speaks to experience, memory and hope." The arc of the truthful universe is long, but it bends toward reality.

Only Connect

Being clear about boundaries and priorities is ordinary wisdom in an organization. Good fences make good neighbors and preserve a sense of place. But being reflexively exclusionary—of talent, of ideas, of opportunities—is a "self-own" that backfires, creating unnecessary disadvantages for the enterprise. When differences are penalized because they are different—whether color or gender, style or standing, culture or capability—alienation supersedes authenticity, and humanness takes it in the ear.

At the other extreme, overconnected and over-inclusive organizations where everyone seems to be in on everything, spawn enmeshed relationships, smother individuality, and violate personal space. Call this a connection to chaos, or absorption in a crowd—which is no connection at all. In a healthy, connected organization, these extremes are avoided. People appreciate being joined with each other and with the larger whole, rooted in the truth of their experience and drawn to higher callings. Hopeful connection combines a grasp of reality with relatedness to people, and it proceeds through phases.

On World Youth Day celebrated in Portugal in 2023, the late Pope Francis said, "There is space for everyone [in the church], and when there isn't, please, let's work so that there is—also for who makes mistakes, for who falls, for whom it is difficult." Then he asked the crowd of young people to repeat after him, "Todos, todos, todos!" Everyone, everyone, everyone!

To end where we began this chapter, the meaning of E.M. Forster's oft-quoted line from his novel, *Howard's End*— "Only connect … " so we may "live in fragments no longer"—is as deep as Pope Francis' message and as layered as our plea to Establish Connection. Forster wanted to bridge what is divided and strive for wholeness in every dimension of our lives. To harmonize hope, connect minds to hearts, persons to persons, and cultures to cultures, and align with truth. Todos!

EIGHT
Who Hopeful Leaders Are

> "The secret of our success is that we never, never give up."
>
> Wilma Mankiller, first woman to be Chief of the Cherokee Nation

Four qualities necessary for the leader who leads from hope emerged consistently in our interviews: optimism, courage, authenticity, and perseverance. They work together like the four points of a compass to orient a leader toward hope.

Optimism

"Optimism is not blind positivity. It is the undying belief that the future is bright," according to Simon Sinek, leadership writer best known for the mantra, "Start with Why." Optimism is one of hope's closest companions; it is neither denial nor naïveté but instead the deliberate choice to focus on what could go right without ignoring what could go wrong. Hopeful leaders cultivate that choice daily. They see beyond obstacles to patterns and potential. "Having someone help us see the possibility at times when we can't see the forest for the trees sparks the imagination," one respondent said. Another described optimism as "oxygen for the group, invisible until it's gone."

Optimism can be contagious when it is real. Wilma Mankiller once said that her role as Chief of the Cherokee Nation was "to remind people that we have survived worse and that we still have the power to shape our future." Her optimism was grounded in memory, not fantasy, rooted in centuries of endurance, and the belief that history gives rise to renewal when people act with intention.

Hopeful leaders know that optimism, like hope itself, requires evidence they help create. They offer small wins, visible progress, and shared meaning that builds confidence. Their optimism is disciplined. It looks squarely at the hard facts, then asks: "What might still be possible here?"

Courage

"Hope lies in dreams, in imagination, and in the courage of those who dare to make dreams into reality," said Jonas Salk, developer of the polio vaccine. Courage is the muscle that gives hope its strength under pressure. It is the willingness to act without guarantees. Brené Brown writes that "hope is borne of courage." To lead from hope is to lead from the possible and to take a step when the path is still forming beneath your feet. It takes courage to see uncertainty as opportunity rather than threat.

Senator John McCain, who endured five and a half years as a prisoner of war, said, "If you do the thing you think you cannot do, you'll feel your hope, your dignity, and your courage grow stronger." His insight is universal. Courage does not erase fear; it places purpose above it.

In our interviews, one executive recalled the first time she spoke truth to her board about the company's cultural failures. "My voice shook," she said, "but I did it anyway. And something shifted. They saw I wasn't blaming. I was believing we could do better." That is hopeful courage—not bravado, but moral clarity in motion.

Authenticity

Before "authentic" meant genuine, it meant being authoritative: something bearing the authority of its origin. Hopeful leaders derive authority from that place. Their influence comes not from role or title, but from congruence between what they say and who they are. Authenticity is magnetic because it frees others to show up whole. When leaders are real, people exhale. One respondent told us, "My team trusts me because I don't hide what I don't know. I name it. And that gives them permission to do the same."

Hopeful leaders are transparent about uncertainty without transmitting fear. They show respect for difference and curiosity for what they might learn from it. Their confidence in the future is rooted in honesty about the present. Parker Palmer calls this, "living divided no more." Authentic leaders stop trying to perform a version of themselves. They act from their center, not from their résumé. When followers sense that congruence in voice, values, and actions aligned, they listen differently. Authenticity becomes a quiet covenant of trust: You can believe me, because I believe what I am saying.

Perseverance

Hopeful leaders are not easily deterred. They are in it for the long haul. Perseverance is the endurance of purpose: the capacity to keep showing up when the outcome remains uncertain. Thomas Jefferson described explorer Meriwether Lewis as a man of "undaunted courage, which nothing but impossibilities could divert from its direction." Jefferson understood that perseverance fuses courage with steadiness. It is what connects hope to action.

Perseverance does not mean rigidity. It means adapting without losing heart. One hospital administrator described the first months of the Covid crisis in this way: "Every day the plan changed, and every night I had to walk the halls and remind people that we were learning, not failing." Her persistence became her team's stability.

Wilma Mankiller embodied that same endurance in a different context. When she took office as Principal Chief in 1985, she faced resistance from within her own community. "I learned that change is hard," she said, "but we keep going because our ancestors kept going." Her perseverance was both cultural and personal, and a reminder that hope has deep roots. To persevere is to protect the fragile beginnings of possibility until they take hold. Hopeful leaders know that the future doesn't arrive fully formed; it grows through persistence—one decision, one conversation, one long day at a time.

The Inner Landscape

Hopeful leadership begins within. Leaders cannot create steadiness around them if they do not cultivate it inside themselves. Emotional regulation—the ability to stay present when the heat rises—is the unspoken foundation of hope. Hopeful are able to notice and name their emotional states before reacting to others. They pause. They breathe. They replace judgment with curiosity. Their calm becomes a signal to the system that the sky is not falling. When others panic, they stay open. When others rush to conclusions, they listen. Their steadiness keeps others steady.

This inner discipline is not detachment; it is engagement with perspective. Hopeful leaders use reflection as fuel. They recover quickly from setbacks because they know the difference between a mistake and a verdict. They learn, adapt, and keep the larger picture in view.

The Social Effect

Hope travels between people when it wells up inside them. Hopeful leaders generate hope through the spaces they create and the tone they set. They build trust through consistent follow-through, and they generate momentum by naming and celebrating progress. People described hopeful leaders as those who "make others more hopeful by how they listen." They pay attention to what is said and unsaid, to the energy in a room, to those who have not yet spoken. They turn attention into inclusion.

When things go wrong, hopeful leaders do not rush to blame. They ask, "What did we learn?" They demonstrate that failure is tuition paid, not evidence of futility. Hope spreads not by proclamation but by practice. It is caught more than taught.

The Legacy

Hopeful leaders think beyond their own tenure. Their measure is not applause but continuity. They build systems, relationships, and habits that keep hope alive after they leave. They invest in others' capacity for hope—mentoring, teaching, and delegating in ways that expand confidence and skill. They plant seeds of belonging, integrity, and shared agency. When they move on, the culture remains strong. Their legacy is not a monument or a quotation; it is a living pattern of resilience. The organizations they touch retain an appetite for learning, an instinct for possibility, and a memory of trust. Hope becomes institutionalized, not idolized.

- Optimism sees the horizon.
- Courage takes the first step toward it.
- Authenticity keeps the journey honest.
- Perseverance carries it through.
- Inner steadiness keeps the compass true.
- Social connection turns hope into a shared resource.
- Legacy ensures hope outlasts the leader.

These are not traits to display but disciplines to practice. Hopeful leaders understand that hope is a way of being—clear-eyed, relational, and enduringly human.

NINE
What Hopeful Leaders Do

"Hope is an attitude in action."

James Kouzes and Barry Posner, leadership scholars and
authors of *The Leadership Challenge :
How to Make Extraordinary Things Happen in Organizations*

Massachusetts Institute of Technology leadership professor, Peter Senge, writes that a leader's attention is never neutral. "It either brings life or it drains it." What you attend to as a leader you amplify. Day to day leadership actions are the threads that bring hope to life.

From *Putting Hope to Work*:

Our study of effective leaders has uncovered many ways in which their decisions, words, and actions make the people they lead more hopeful. Collectively, these practices are the basis of a leadership toolkit for building and sustaining hope.

But the most important change comes when a leader is simply more mindful of this vital part of their mission. Much can be accomplished in a reflective pause to ask, "Is what I am about to say or do likely to be destructive or accretive of hope?"

When we asked people to tell us specifically about actions that had a hopeful effect, there was great consistency in the patterns they described.

Listening, Hearing and Responding

Listening is where hope begins. It opens possibilities and reveals a larger world. It is one thing to listen, another thing to hear, and still another to show you have heard by acting. Hopeful leaders do all three. They listen not only to the individual but also to the team, creating open, participative processes that invite genuine input. From that sense of inclusion, hope takes root. My voice matters, my presence counts. As Robert Greenleaf, founder of the "servant leadership" movement, observed the first duty of a leader is to serve, and the first duty of a servant is to listen. True service begins in attention: the willingness to set aside one's own agenda long enough to hear what another person is trying to say.

In a world where time is money, the gift of attention becomes a powerful act of respect and care. When people feel heard, they are validated; when they are validated, they contribute; and when they contribute, both they and the organization grow stronger. M. Scott Peck, author of *The Road Less Traveled: A New Psychology of Love, Traditional Values, and Spiritual Growth*, called such attention the essence of caring. To truly attend to someone, to listen fully, is to recognize their humanity. Listening, in that sense, is not a technique but a gift of self.

In a similar vein, Ellen Langer, a pioneering researcher on mindfulness—the active awareness of context and perspective—has shown how mindful listening benefits leaders. Staying receptive rather than defensive and curious rather than certain, keeps possibility alive and reminds us that caring is not passive. Caring is an active stance toward others and toward a future we are trying to build together.

To listen is to lead with hope. It says, you matter, this moment matters. Listening is not a pause before action. Listening is the action that changes what happens next. When people are heard, they rise. When leaders listen with care and curiosity, possibility expands, and hope becomes audible.

Providing Context

Context is our lens on experience. Gregory Bateson, the anthropologist and systems theorist, said that, "Without context, words and actions have no meaning at all." It shapes the meanings we make and the actions we take. Hopeful contexts empower, shedding light on possibilities and opportunities from the leader's vantage point. Particularly in situations where people cannot see the forest for the trees because they are too anxious, overwhelmed, or stuck, the alert leader can boost hope by reframing the context and adjusting the lens.

Leaders who have been in the trenches can draw on their experience and longevity. They know appearances can mislead, and that somewhere there exists an opportunity. A turn of phrase can reframe a negative into a positive and show how pieces connect to the overall vision. Keeping the big picture front and center reenergizes hope, according to this manager:

> Most of us get pulled down into the day to day. What's going wrong now? We're not really hopeless; we're just stuck in neutral. We're wired to be detailed. We need to see how the daily connects to something bigger.

Providing context helps people make meaning of a situation in ways that are more productive, inspiring, empowering, and forward-looking. When a doctor lays out a diagnosis and a course of treatment for a patient, hope is enhanced and the effectiveness of the treatment is increased. Similarly, when a leader provides perspective, it builds a framework for action, a way to understand experience. Wilfred Drath and Charles Palus, researchers at the Center for Creative Leadership, write that leadership is a "process of making sense of what people are doing together so that people will understand and be committed." Hopeful leaders invite people to look at situations in positive, opportunistic ways by providing context. The facts do not change. What changes is what people believe they can do.

Saying Three Little Words

The organizational psychologist Amy Edmondson writes, "Psychological safety is a belief that the context is safe for interpersonal risk-taking—that speaking up with new ideas, questions, concerns, or mistakes will be welcomed and valued even when I'm wrong." In an organizational context, saying "I don't know" is powerful. But uttering those three little words can be risky where people are expected to have all the answers. Here is a leader describing a common situation:

> I encourage my reports to say, "I don't know." I believe it for myself, but it's harder when I get into a meeting with my boss even though he says it's OK not to know. He means it, but it's very hard for people to say it. There's that underlying feeling that we should know.

> One of our respondents told us of a manager who introduced the notion of "I don't know, but I'll get back to you." People were not

bringing her the truth." The obvious downside of admitting you don't know is that it exposes you and makes you vulnerable. "I don't know," is the gift of truth, and where there is truth, there is hope.

Championing Learning

British organizational learning theorist Reg Revans offered a deceptively simple equation with biological roots. For any living system to survive, its rate of learning must be equal to or greater than the rate of change in its environment. When learning lags behind, extinction begins. In a fast-changing world, leaders cannot promise stability, but they can cultivate adaptability. Learning becomes the lifeline. Edmondson notes that "a learning frame is not only healthier, it's also more rational than a performance frame. It's more in tune with the uncertainty and constant challenges found in any life or job." A performance frame looks backward, and asks: "How well did we do?" A learning frame looks beyond results and asks, "What does this teach us? What can we try next?"

Hopeful leaders live in that forward frame. They know that mistakes are the raw material of excellence. When things go wrong, they ask, "How can we build on what has happened?" They understand that when a mistake occurs, the tuition has already been paid.

Learning cultures start with curiosity, and curiosity thrives where psychological safety exists. When people trust that candor is not a risk, they are more likely to tell what they know. They can say, "We tried, it didn't work, here's what we found…." In such settings, failure becomes fuel. Progress is built on insight, not perfection. Organizations that excel at learning make it routine.

Hope and learning move together. Hopeful leaders champion learning continuously. They act with humility and remind others that growth behinds where certainty ends. People feel freer to act, to test, to risk. They are moved to act on the belief that what they learn today can make tomorrow better. The essence of hope is the conviction that effort, guided by insight, can shape the future.

Storytelling

Stories are how human beings make sense of change. Before we had data, we had narrative. Before we had maps, we had myths. Stephen Denning, former World Bank executive, learned this the hard way. Tasked with mobilizing a vast global organization for transformation, he tried logic, process, and persuasion. None of it worked. Then he told a story about a small project in Africa that solved a local problem through knowledge sharing, and people listened. "Storytelling," he later wrote, "was the only thing that worked." Denning calls stories "round-edged"—they slide into our minds more easily than facts, and they stay there longer. A good story is portable; people can repeat it, adapt it, and make it their own.

Stories are the glue of community and the fabric of connection. They preserve the past and illuminate the path forward. They carry values, signal belonging and transmit hope across time. Every healthy organization runs on stories. Some are "official," and some are not—told backstage, around the watercooler, or whispered, perhaps told when the official story is no longer true. Stories explain who we are, what we value, and why it matters.

Hopeful, innovative communities are rich in what might be called operationally enabling stories. These are stories that instruct as they inspire. They show how people overcame obstacles, took smart risks, and learned together. They give courage by reminding us that others have stood in this uncertain place before and found a way through. Leaders who understand this use story as a tool of coherence and possibility. They gather and retell stories that connect the daily grind to the greater purpose. They listen for new stories rising in the organization These are often stories of resilience, discovery, and care. Rather than impose meaning, they help meaning emerge.

Hope grows through story because stories give shape to experience. They turn confusion into pattern, isolation into belonging, effort into legacy. The hopeful leader knows that every story told well, and every honest account of what was tried, learned, or redeemed, becomes a seed of the future.

Assessing Progress

Hopeful leaders understand that process is as important as outcome. They know how people work together matters as much as what they achieve. Chris Argyris, pioneer of organizational learning, taught that real progress begins when people examine not only their results but also their reasoning. Argyris called this "double-loop learning." In the first loop, people identify what went wrong and make adjustments—the familiar cycle of problem solving and correction. In the second loop, they step back to ask a deeper question: "What assumptions led us to act this way in the first place?" Progress, he said, depends on testing the thinking behind our actions, not just the actions themselves.

This practice turns assessment into inquiry. Instead of looking for someone to blame, a double-loop conversation explores the beliefs, expectations, and habits that shaped behavior. It makes learning visible. Over time, people become more candid, less defensive, and more capable of self-correction. They notice patterns, how decisions are made, how conflict is avoided, and how authority is used or withheld.

When leaders assess progress in this way, they validate the process of learning and show that reflection is a sign of strength, not weakness. Progress is rarely a straight line; it bends, circles, and sometimes doubles back. What matters is that people stay engaged, curious, and willing to learn.

Assessment without blame builds confidence and capability. It turns review into renewal. Instead of asking who fell short, hopeful leaders ask what the experience revealed and what can be done differently next time. This simple shift in posture transforms performance into practice, and mistakes into material for improvement. When people see that their effort is noticed and their learning is valued, they take more initiative. They ask questions, try again, and look ahead. The organization grows more adaptable and its people more self-assured. Hope thrives where judgment gives way to discernment, and where evaluation is not a verdict but an invitation to grow.

Creating and Holding Space

Hope thrives in open space. It withers under rigidity, over-control, and the weight of too many rules. Space allows for imagination and movement. It gives people permission to breathe, explore, and try, and they resonate with the phrase "elbow room." Many of the most hopeful stories we heard came from work that was new, pioneering, and oriented toward discovery and growth. People find energy in uncharted waters, in initiatives or phases of work where the path is not already worn.

- Hope is easier in a creative phase; everything is new.
- There is a spark of energy and engagement in possibility.
- You are hope-filled instead of stuck in routine or dulled by complacency.

Hopeful leaders create and hold space for exploration, thinking time, and open conversation. They understand that space itself is a form of leadership. It signals trust. It gives people permission to shape, question and imagine. Making space means allowing others to find their footing instead of rushing to define it for them.

Creating space also means designing organizations with enough flexibility to learn and grow. When systems run too lean, there is no slack for reflection, recovery, or reinvention. Efficiency without margin suffocates imagination. A certain amount of redundancy in roles is not wasteful, it is wise. It allows people to back one another up, to experiment, and innovate. That bit of extra capacity creates room for "blue ocean" initiatives, for ideas that move beyond the known map. It is the excess that leads to success.

Holding space is a quiet discipline. It is not the absence of direction but the presence of attention. It means staying open when uncertainty rises, protecting the creative process before it hardens into habit, and resisting the impulse to fill every silence. Hope needs air. It grows where there is room to think, speak, and imagine together. Leaders who hold this kind of space do more than protect it; they model it. They show that patience and presence are not delays but forms of wisdom. They invite others into the creative tension between what is and what might be. In that space, discovery unfolds, and people remember what it feels like to be fully alive at work.

Hiring and Promoting the "Right" People

"So much of what hope is about is the right people," one leader told us. Hope at work depends on people willing to embrace the five principles and put them into practice. Hope is nurtured when you see leaders acting in visible, obvious, genuine ways that are in keeping with the culture they claim to value. Hope is contagious when behavior and belief align. It falters when there is a gap between what is said and what is done. People read those gaps quickly. They can tell when vision is performative and when it is lived. The most hopeful organizations make that alignment visible through daily conduct, not slogans.

Hiring and promotion decisions carry more influence over hope than most leaders realize. Every new hire and every appointment can reinforce or weaken the shared sense of purpose. Hope rides in the balance when people ask, sometimes quietly, "Will this person make us stronger, fairer, more genuine?" The answer is not found in credentials or charisma but in values-based fit.

In hopeful organizations, fit is not about sameness or cultural comfort. It is about integrity. Fit means personal and organizational values are in conversation, not in conflict. It means people can bring their "rageddy" selves to work without pretending to be someone else. When that happens, hope flows naturally. Leaders build hopeful cultures by choosing people who embody what the organization aspires to be and by becoming those people themselves. When the right people are in place, hope becomes a presence not a program.

Monitoring Hope

Robin Sharma, in *The Monk Who Sold His Ferrari: A Fable About Fulfilling Your Dreams and Reaching Your Destiny*, writes, "What you focus on grows, what you think about expands, and what you dwell upon determines your destiny." Hope is no exception. It grows through attention. Monitoring hope is not a program or a quarterly report; it is a constant act of awareness on the part of the leader. Hopeful leaders learn to read the emotional weather of their organizations. They observe, inquire, and listen. They notice tone and body language, silence and energy, the words people choose and the ones they avoid. They study the flow of conversation the way an anthropologist studies culture, looking for meaning beneath habit. They sense when people are leaning in and when they are pulling away. They pay attention to how meetings begin and end, which stories are repeated, which are celebrated, and which are ignored.

Diagnosing hope in a system is both art and discipline. It combines rational, emotional, and intuitive ways of knowing. The rational mind tracks patterns in behavior and performance. The emotional mind perceives tone and tension. The intuitive mind picks up on things not said. Together these perspectives form a fuller, more human picture of how hope lives or falters inside the system.

Monitoring hope also means practicing empathy in both ways that we use the term: accuracy and compassion. Empathic accuracy is the ability to understand what others are feeling—with precision—and to read signals clearly and without projection. Compassionate empathy is the willingness to act on that understanding, and to offer help that is helpful. Without action, empathy becomes observation; with action, it becomes leadership. Hope grows where people feel seen and supported, not studied.

Leaders who monitor hope in this way develop what might be called diagnostic empathy, the capacity to sense when people are stretched too thin, when possibility is closing, or when cynicism begins to replace curiosity. They do not wait for crisis. They tend to hope the way gardeners tend to soil, cultivating the conditions that allow life to take hold again.

Monitoring hope means being alert to signals of vitality or fatigue and responding with courage and compassion. Leaders who practice this form of attention become stewards of hope. They do not simply measure it—they nurture it. They understand that leadership is not only about building the future, but about sustaining belief in its possibility.

TEN

How Leaders Keep Their Hope Alive

> "You are a light. You are the light. Never let anyone—any person or any force— dampen, dim, or diminish your light."
>
> John Lewis, congressman and crusader for justice

When the Dakota Access Pipeline was slated to cut through burial grounds on her land, LaDonna Brave Bull Allard, historian of the Standing Rock Sioux, did not file a brief. She opened her backyard. That patch of prairie became Sacred Stone Camp in 2016, the first outpost of the global resistance to protect the Missouri River. Allard held hope on her homeland. She stood in liminal space, between the pain of violation and the possibility of renewal. Her stance was both protest and prayer. She created room for grief, defiance, and dignity in a circle strong enough to hold them all.

When dogs and pepper spray met the water protectors, she knelt and prayed. Witnesses said the attack stopped. Later she said, "We are our own medicine." Hope for her was never solitary. She invited children to write letters about water and send them into the world. Their words rekindled agency across the movement. "I follow the young people," she said.

Even as the camps were dismantled, she began again, planning a "green village" on her land and teaching that resistance also means building life. Allard drew strength from ceremony, kinship, and memory. She held hope as stewardship for her community. Hopeful leaders like Allard are both flame and vessel. They hold the tension between despair and creation.

The Balanced Container

Consider, at both a visceral and spiritual level, the demanding work hopeful leaders do and the enormous outflow of energy it takes. Leaders often provide emotional and moral ballast for their teams. As one respondent said, "You can't give energy without getting energy back." Hopeful leadership is an act of endurance and a sustained practice of renewal.

The leaders we speak of are ambassadors of possibility. One invisible but critical function they perform is what we call holding the container: creating, sustaining and protecting a space where transformative human energy can emerge. Within that space, people can risk new ideas, voice uncertainty, and take part in shaping a future that does not yet exist.

The hopeful leader, as a change agent, stands with one foot in today and one in tomorrow. "Standing in the tragic gap," Parker Palmer calls it, and "holding the tension between the reality of the moment and the possibility that something better might emerge." Maintaining this stance requires stamina, personal belief, and courage. Palmer admits,

"I harbor no illusions about how hard it is to live in that gap. Though we may try to keep our grip on both reality and hope, sometimes the tension is too hard to hold."

The Hope Bucket

In our interviews, many leaders confessed that this stance can be exhausting. One executive described it as, "carrying the flame into the wind." Another said, "When I lose hope, it's never all at once; it leaks out slowly, in small compromises of what I know to be possible."

Maintaining a hopeful stance during those times when "you're digging hard to find it" requires constant attention to and care for one's inner life. "Constantly I have to replenish my supply of hope." Balance is essential: "My strength is recognizing when positive and negative are getting out of balance." As soon as the scale starts tipping, this leader acts to restore equilibrium.

The beginning of replenishment is paying attention. As important as monitoring hope in the organization is remembering to take your pulse. "Where your attention goes, your energy flows," says the life coach Tony Robbins. A seasoned manager told us: "If I don't have hope myself, I step back, get better perspective, perhaps realize I had false hope, or that my expectations were unrealistic. I reassess my objectives, and that usually generates more hope."

Taking your pulse also means listening and trusting what you hear. When the warning lights flash, you pause. Replenishment begins not with doing more, but with noticing. A leader who is running on empty cannot be a catalyst for hope. Hope must flow through a well-tended vessel. The next step is developing a rich assortment of ways to refill your hope bucket. These are not luxuries—they are lifelines.

Consider Coaching

Coaches come in many forms: supervisors, colleagues, mentors, partners, professionals. What matters is trust. One leader recalled, "My best coach was a retired colleague who had nothing to prove. He would just listen, then ask, 'What do you want to be true a year from now?' That question re-centered me every time."

A good coach holds a mirror without judgment and sees your strength when you have misplaced it. The coaching relationship itself becomes a small container of hope, one conversation at a time. But what is most important in coaching, as in a therapeutic or even friend-to-friend relationship, is that you care for one another. Care engenders hope.

Build Networks and Sustain Relationships

Isolation is the enemy of hope. Being on the edge of change can be lonely, and without companions, the view from that edge can be distorted. The leaders we admire curate their circles carefully. They surround themselves with people who hold similar values and remind them who they are when they forget. One nonprofit director said, "I have a small tribe that believes in me even when my confidence wavers. They don't fix things; they hold me until I can see clearly again."

Reconnect Body and Mind

Health, rest, humor, and play are not indulgences, they are preconditions for perspective. Nearly every leader we interviewed mentioned some practice of quieting the mind.

- I've found you really need to take care of yourself to maintain a clear-eyed view of possibility.
- When I'm healthier, not so exhausted, I'm more hopeful.

- I started yoga to cope with the cacophony in my head. It did a lot to quiet my mind.
- For me, to know hope is present, I have to quiet my mind. I listen to the still, small voice.

The body reminds us that leadership energy is not endless—and that it requires daily renewal. One university dean described her morning walks: "At sunrise, everything looks possible again. I can feel my perspective expanding with the light."

Focus on Others

Wise words from *How Can I Help: Stories and Reflections on Service*, by two social justice activists and practitioners of compassionate service, Ram Dass and Paul Gorman: "We work on ourselves, then, in order to help others. And we help others as a vehicle for helping ourselves." Service is one of the surest paths back to hope. When leaders turn outward to mentor, encourage or simply notice others, they heal.

Mark Gibson, a retired physician and healthcare executive recalls how he would re-center and self-soothe after an adverse medical event. He would sit by a patient and hold their hand. Patient and doctor help each other. Others said:

- Hope and help are intertwined.
- I focus on the young people who report to me, seeing them grow. I want them to do really well. I can make a difference by sharing things I've learned and helping them get recognized.
- In times when I can't find my own sense of hope, it helps to help someone else find theirs.

In the act of helping, we transcend the self's limits and rejoin the flow of giving and receiving that sustains community.

The Practice of Renewal

Each of us sustains hope in a uniquely personal way. For some it is silence, for others, movement or laughter or prayer. The point is to find a reliable way of restoring inner equilibrium. A hopeful leader is not a reservoir of positivity but a conduit, constantly exchanging energy with the world. You are the light, as John Lewis reminds us. Hope needs protection, refueling and deliberate tending. To lead with hope is to commit to personal renewal. Fill your bucket before you give again. Hold the container steady while others find their footing. Remember that the flame of possibility you carry burns brightest when it lights the way for others. Remember too, as LaDonna Allard said, "We are our own medicine."

ELEVEN
Tracking Signs of Hope at Work

> "Hope is often about action rather than feeling; it's the knowledge that what we do matters, even when it's hard to see results."
>
> Jane Goodall, primatologist and conservationist

Management lore says: "People don't do what you *expect—they do what you inspect*." True enough when expectations are vague or contradictory. We might say, be clear about what you want your group to achieve, or you will be disappointed. Yet "too much" inspection can invite transactional behavior at the cost of commitment. Hopeful leaders look deeper and see more. They know that:

- What you inspect tends to happen.
- What you attend to may improve.
- What you celebrate can multiply.

Hopeful leadership shifts the gaze from fault-finding to possibility-seeking, and from catching errors to noticing effort and progress. When leaders practice attention and celebration, the message that lands is what everyone wants to hear: I see you. What you do, matters. You belong.

In Martin Seligman's words, hope is both a motor—fueling effort, persistence and imagination—and a meter—a gauge of what lies under the surface. Hope trackers stay present to what matters! They read the meter while tending the motor.

How to Begin

Now pretend for a moment that you are an anthropologist from Mars. Walk into your organization as if for the first time. You are there to do observational research. You are looking for clues, cues, patterns that reveal whether hope is at work. What do you notice? What draws your attention? Hope leaves tracks.

Skilled trackers call it "dirt time": slowing down to see what is right in front of you. Fine-tune your senses. Look with fresh eyes at familiar ground. The signs of hope are almost always there if you choose to look for them. Tracking hope requires you to pay close attention to the daily habits that create culture. Chances are, people are not using the word "hope," even if their practices are grounded in principles of hope. According to one leader, "I'm struck by how rarely I use the word, but how true it is to my work and why I stay connected here."

The practice of becoming an anthropologist requires beginning with an open mind and a broad lens. How do you know when hope is present? In yourself? In others? In this place? There are outward and visible signs. "Those of us who keep our eyes open can read volumes in what we see going on around us," writes the cultural anthropologist, Edward T. Hall. The signs of hope are everywhere. Your job, if you choose to accept it, is to pay attention!

Start with a Broad Scan

The late Charles Handy, the Irish philosopher and management theorist, characterized an organization with spirit and soul much as our interviewees described the hopeful organization. You can see it and feel it the moment you walk in the door or when you meet someone who works there. For Handy, such places abound in what he calls the "E factors": energy, enthusiasm, effort, excitement, and excellence. The talk is in the first-person plural— "we," not "they"—and the organization stands for something beyond profit: "something grander, something worthy of one's commitment, skills, and time." Hope at work shows up in how people appear, what they say, and how they work.

Notice How People Appear

Hope has a silent, behavioral language. You can see it in attitude, energy, work ethic, language, affect. You can see it in the light in someone's eyes. You can hear it in a voice alive with energy and passion or in laughter. The eyes are the window to the soul, according to the adage, and a window into hope. In the words of one observant manager: "I know by the light that sits behind someone's eyes. Instead of nodding yes, they're thinking yes."

People spoke of eyes "coming alive" or getting bigger. From the eyes, hope moves to "the whole face, animated, coming to life." The voice too, comes to life "with energy and passion—no flat emotional tone." The whole body is energized. As one leader who had succeeded in rescuing a business said: "You can physically see it—the spring in a person's step. When I first came to this organization, people were beaten down, ignored, victims. No hope. Now they've started smiling again, laughing, not that tight look on their faces." According to another respondent, "Hope in a company either is there or it is not. When it is, you can see it in your people in their attitude, behavior, work ethic, on their faces, in their language, in their eyes, in their step." This is hope's silent, behavioral language, according to another person:

> You know that hope is present because you can feel it emotionally, physically, spiritually and intellectually. It is not something easily described, but you can feel it at the very core of your being. You can see and experience it in others. Hope is authentic and cannot be faked. It shows up in how you and others act, in what is done and said. You can observe it in a presentation, in meetings and in how people interact. You can see it in the written word by reading between the lines.

Listen to What People Say

As you walk the halls or sit in a meeting, listen closely to the level of positive talk, a key indicator of whether hope is alive and well. Positive talk is confident, can-do, forward-looking, inclusive of people and ideas, tolerant, energetic, realistic, and honest. True positive talk, in good or bad times, indicates true hope. On the other hand, true negative talk indicates what Rosamund Stone Zander and Benjamin Zander write about in *The Art of Possibility: Transforming Professional and Personal Life*. They describe "downward spiral talk … a resigned way of speaking that excludes possibility." Upward spiral talk is expansive and freeing.

Watch How People Work

Hope at work manifests itself in people's attitudes towards their work and their interactions with others. What connects the two is a heightened sense of personal commitment and responsibility, not only to me and my job, but to the whole, the community, the team. High-hope teams share three traits:

- They balance inquiry and advocacy.
- They balance attention to others with focus on self.
- They overweight the positive.

When we feel hope our confidence in ourselves and others grows. Hope in action is a flexible, dynamic force that helps us overcome difficult challenges because, like reality, hope is not static. Hope constantly monitors reality and adjusts expectations accordingly.

Now Take a Closer Look

Use the five principles as a diagnostic tool to take a hope pulse, starting with you and extending to the team and organization. Only with an honest look inward can there be an honest look outward. If you know your relationship to the five principles, you are less likely to filter out conflicting signals. Ask yourself these questions first, then include the teams you work with: (Please resist the urge to turn this inquiry into a survey. These are questions for listening, reflection, and dialogue.)

a. When have you felt hope at work?
b. What made that possible?

Possibility

Remember a time you/we were really inspired by a possibility. Why is it so memorable? To what extent do you/we feel a sense of shared possibility? Can you/we envision a worthwhile goal you/we are excited about moving forward on, together?

Agency

Do you/we feel a sense of agency? Do you/we have enough of a voice to make a valued contribution? Can you/we make things happen with action and influence? Are you/we involved soon enough? Are ownership, responsibility, and involvement distributed among those who need to make things happen?

Worth

Do you/we know and experience our worth in terms of its meaning and contribution of our work to the greater good? Is personal purpose aligned with organizational purpose and values? Is there a clear line of sight to our stakeholders and customers? Are you/we operating from our strengths?

Openness

Are you/we given the grace to learn? Is there openness to question assumptions? Is it safe to speak the truth of one's experience? Is there comfort being open to outcomes and welcoming to surprises? Is there elbow room to innovate? Can you/we challenge legacies, sacred cows, and powerful paradigms?

Connection

Do you/we feel connected in all the ways that matter? Are you/we connecting to each other? To your/our team? To the context? To both personal and collective purpose? To truth and to reality? To the needs of those we serve? Is there patience for dialogue and meaning making? Are safety and belonging valued?

Viewing results through the lens of the principles reveals the "why" beneath what we achieve. For teams, reflection aligns focus on actionable insights and cultivates hopeful culture.

Becoming an Anthropologist

"The first act of leadership is to notice," writes Peter Block, author and community builder. The signs of hope are everywhere if you learn to pay attention. Approach your workplace as an anthropologist would, with curiosity, patience, and perhaps a notebook in hand. Observe the rituals, the hallway conversations, the laughter and silences. Notice what is there, what is missing, and where people's eyes light up. Track the patterns both as a participant and as an observer, inside the circle and at its edge. Once you know how to recognize and track hope, you can harness it and design systems and practices that allow hope to thrive.

This is what we know, as Octavio Paz, poet and Nobel laureate has said: "Anyone who has looked Hope in the face will never forget it. He will search for it everywhere he goes … and he will dream of finding it again."

TWELVE
Putting Hope to Work—Again

> "The Hope Gap is the dangerous belief that change isn't possible."
>
> Afdhel Aziz, author and social impact strategist

Around the globe, a widening divide separates what people fear from what they still believe they can change. Nearly seven in ten people say they are worried about the future. Fewer than four in ten believe the world will be better in five years. This is the "Hope Gap"—the emotional distance between anxiety and agency. It grows when stories highlight crisis without showing progress, when despair is amplified, and when renewal is ignored. Hopeful leadership begins by closing that gap, day by day.

Hope as Survival

Jane Goodall calls hope "a crucial survival trait that has sustained our species from the time of our Stone Age ancestors." Hope is not sentimental; it is adaptive. It has always been a way of orienting toward life. It kept early humans searching for food, light, and safety. Goodall often said that without hope, people do nothing. Hope is necessary for making meaning, pursuing justice, and enduring as a species. When leaders draw upon that instinct—to persist, to imagine, to build—they revive something ancient and essential. To abandon hope is to deny a defining feature of being human.

Hope as Strategy

Douglas Anweiler, a strategy consultant who endorses hope, writes: "Hope is where strategy and story meet. It's the narrative foundation that makes strategic action possible. When you choose hope, you're not ignoring reality; you're deciding which reality you're going to work toward." Hope in this sense is disciplined. It does not avoid hard truths. It works with them. It demands clear-eyed assessment paired with deliberate choice. Hope is strategy in its purest form—a commitment to shape the future, not submit to it.

Hope in Action

Anweiler reports this example of what we mean by hope in the work of the Canadian Cystic Fibrosis Treatment Society as they fought for access to Trikafta, a life-changing therapy for people living with CF.

> After a year of stalemate between governments and pharmaceutical companies, the pressure to quit was real. Founder and Chair Chris MacLeod, who lives with CF himself, voiced what many felt—it might be time to move on. Instead, the Society chose hope. They did not retreat. They kept fighting in courtrooms, in the media, and in the hearts of families across Canada. A year later, Trikafta was approved. The campaign

did more than win. It changed the narrative. It built momentum, reshaped public will and helped save lives.

That is what hope as strategy looks like. Not naïve. Not passive. Courageous, coordinated, and sustained.

Habits of Hope

Our aim in this book is to show how hope can be understood, strengthened, and practiced. The five principles—Uphold Worth, Establish Connection, Explore Possibility, Activate Agency, and Embrace Openness—offer a framework for doing that work every day. But to close the Hope Gap, we must continue to demonstrate that hope works. Leaders do this by making a choice that makes every other choice possible: the choice to act from hope.

Our choice is to pass the baton. We are now creating, *Hope at Work: A Guide to Habits That Make a Difference.* For fifty years we have curated a family of practices that breathe life into organizations by putting the five principles to work. We call them habits because they are the small, repeatable actions that shape how we work together day by day. Their accumulation becomes our culture. These practices are not a program or a season. They are a way of life.

Our guide is intended to help you facilitate and ground your own leadership of hope. We see it as placing the baton in your hands—a handoff from our generation to yours. We pass it on to you with gratitude and conviction. The race is not over. The work of hope continues.

We Never Left

We reaffirm hope because the times demand it. Hope turns vision into movement, effort into progress, and people into a community. Hope is alive in how people treat one another and how they face what is next.

When hope is practiced, work has purpose and the future has shape. What has been said before needs to be said again, and again: **Hope at work makes a better future possible.**

WITH GRATITUDE

The process of requesting and receiving endorsements from colleagues, leaders, scholars, practitioners, and influencers across sectors and generations has been a joyful capstone to our two years of inquiry and writing. Each voice offers a distinct entry point into *Hope at Work* shaped by lived experience and reflective practice. We are deeply appreciative to all.

We are also grateful to people with whom we had conversations and interviews but whose names do not appear in the book. They include Howard Behar, Cliff Burrows, Kate Cowie, Gail Civille, Michael Conforti, Carmen Garrett-Goodwine, Troy Geesaman, Joe Gottschalk, Sandra Janoff, Martha Johnson, Juan Lacey, Ron Lambert, Tyler Nash, Cathy Pagliaro, Francesca Peri, Lisa Reynolds, Mike Ritz, Calvin Royal, Virginia Tenpenny, Traci York. Apologies if we missed someone—everyone on this project has been kind and undeservedly generous.

As former public-school teachers, we know impact matters more than intent. Ever curious, we searched for patterns in the endorsements, and we found three consistent themes: First, hope is a disciplined and strategic leadership practice that can be cultivated, embedded, and sustained in organizational life. Second, hope functions as a bridge between uncertainty and action, enabling individuals and organizations to face realities while moving forward with agency and purpose. Third, hope is fundamentally relational: It is created through interpersonal connection. Hope comes alive when people feel seen, valued, and capable of shaping what comes next.

May hope move from our pages to your practice.

BARBARA PERRY

Barbara Perry, Ph.D., is a cultural anthropologist who has advised the tribes we call organizations for 50 years. Her work, rooted in the intersection of culture, organizational learning, and hope, has been applied to a wide variety of organizational challenges from innovation to large scale systemic transformation.

As a teacher, her goal is to stimulate growth in systems and individuals by designing processes that honor and integrate individual voice with collective knowledge and aligned action, to create resilient organizations capable of thriving in chaotic and complex times.

Her previous writing includes articles on using team ethnography to uncover customer needs, the start-up of a high-performance work system, organizational learning, and the book, *Putting Hope to Work: Five Principles to Activate your Organization's Most Powerful Resource.*

HARRY HUTSON

Harry Hutson, Ph.D., is a leadership development professional who works with organizations worldwide, as a coach, consultant, and educator. Earlier in his career, he held senior human resources and organizational development roles at Cummins, Avery Dennison, Global Knowledge, and Devon Energy.

Known for his blend of curiosity and care, he helps people "get out of their own way" and build cultures of meaningful accomplishment.

His professional publications are designed for reflective, purpose-driven leaders. His books include *Putting Hope to Work Five Principles to Activate your Organization's Most Powerful Resource; Navigating an Organizational Crisis: When Leadership Matters Most;* and *Leadership in Nonprofit Organizations.*

www.ingramcontent.com/pod-product-compliance
Lightning Source LLC
Chambersburg PA
CBHW031622210526

45464CB00004B/1704